MORE
THAN ONE MOUNTAIN
TO CLIMB

JOHN GROOMS MISSION STATEMENT
(adopted by the Council of Management in 1993)
reads as follows:

John Grooms is a Christian-based association working in partnership with disabled people to improve their quality of life, to maximise their freedom of choice, to respect their dignity at all times, and to achieve a level of independent living appropriate to their needs and desires.

MORE THAN ONE MOUNTAIN TO CLIMB

The Story of John Grooms
1866 – 1996
and into the future.

By

RUTH E. GILLARD

First published in Great Britain in 1996
by John Grooms Association for Disabled People
50 Scrutton Street, London EC2A 4PH.

ISBN 0 9508094 1 1

We record our special thanks to the family of the late Nancy Martin for permitting the
use of material researched by her for her book 'In a Changing World' published by John
Grooms in 1982.

We acknowledge with thanks the permission granted by 'The Independent' newspaper
to use the abseiling photograph incorporated into the front cover design of this book.

It has been a privilege to have access to an excellent collection of historical and modern
photographs and we gratefully acknowledge the work of –

 A&B Photography
 AIM International
 John Banks
 Nik Bartrum
 Lesley Burke
 David Constantine – Motivation
 Elliot and Fry Ltd
 Chris Fairclough – Packshot
 Melanie Friend
 Gorrod Studios
 Graham Grieves
 Guildhall Picture Library
 Lucie Husband
 Mervyn Lewis – Ashwood Photography
 J P Little
 London Aerial Photo Library
 Michael J O'Brien
 Milton Keynes Photo Services
 Photoscope
 The Review, St Albans
 Seepix
 The Shaftesbury Society
 Derek Tamea
 Tennant Brown Photography
 Turner Gee Studios

We are also grateful for the use of many private photographs and of those of unknown
origin, also sketch drawings by Armes Associates and Peter Kesteven.

The work of the office staff of John Grooms and of the members of the History Book
ad hoc Committee, chaired by Mrs Nancy Robertson MBE, in collating the materials,
records and photographs from which this book has been compiled, is acknowledged
with sincere thanks.

Designed, produced and printed in Great Britain for John Grooms
by Nuprint Limited, Harpenden, Herts. AL5 4SE

CONTENTS

INDEX OF PHOTOGRAPHS AND ILLUSTRATIONS
and acknowledgements to Photographers

Her Royal Highness The Duchess of Kent
PATRON

Dr George Carey, Archbishop of Canterbury
PRESIDENT

FOREWORD

By Dr George Carey, Archbishop of Canterbury

The name of John Groom may not be well known today but he was one of the most significant men of the nineteenth century in bringing about social change. Such were the appalling conditions in which people lived in our cities then, that John Groom was driven to harness his Christian vision of the value of human beings in God's sight to a programme of action which continues to this day.

This book captures the excitement of those early days and reflects the innovative work of the Association in this its 130th year.

John Groom's vision was prophetic, and the Association which bears his name continues to pioneer supportive ways in which disabled people can play a full and active part in contemporary society.

I am proud to be President of this worthwhile charity and hope that through this book many others will want to be associated with a Christian cause which is doing so much good.

Lambeth Palace
London SE1 7JU

March 1996

George Carey

ACKNOWLEDGEMENTS

Whilst researching and writing this book, I have received an enormous amount of help from so many people without whose whole-hearted co-operation the task would have proved almost impossible. A number of them are specifically mentioned by name in the text of the final chapter of the book, but many are not and to you all – John Grooms residents, tenants, staff, volunteers – I say a very warm 'thank you'!

In particular, I owe a considerable debt to the four members of the History Book Ad-hoc Committee so ably chaired by Mrs. Nancy Robertson. They have met at monthly intervals with me throughout most of the year 1995, encouraging me, giving me guidance and supplying historical facts, arranging visits to many of Grooms units, accompanying and taking me round personally, thanks being especially due in this respect to Allan Plumpton, Richard Hale and James Robertson. Committee meetings have contained prayer that I might be inspired and given wisdom and guidance by Almighty God so that the task might be completed to His honour and glory.

DEDICATION

This book is dedicated to Almighty God and to two people who inspired it:

Charles Moore OBE who passed to Glory in 1994 – a man of great character, whose strong Christian faith was the linchpin of his whole life and the motivating force behind all his work – especially at John Grooms (1969 – 1992).

And to **Lorraine Hebditch**, whose warmth of Christian friendship and stoic heroism in the face of physical disability throughout her life has been a great support and encouragement to me.

Ruth E. Gillard
Chertsey, Surrey
March 1996

Aerial view of John Grooms estate at Edgware (1995)

PROLOGUE

I t was the Spring of 1950. Fluffy clouds in the shape of battlements drifted across a clear blue sky. A slight breeze set daffodils nodding and scented the air with the heady perfume of hyacinths. I stepped down from the bus and stood for a few moments enjoying my pleasant surroundings. Ahead of me was a large estate. The office block stood squarely in front, with the larger factory building just beyond. To the right was the long low concert hall and kitchen quarters. The red brick houses I was to know so well were scattered round the grounds, dwarfed to doll size by lovely old trees already showing delicate traceries of greenery.

I had come for an interview: assistant housemother at John Groom's Crippleage, as it was then called. The letter received in answer to my job application had read: 'The girls live in hostels, each having accommodation for twenty-five, and there is a housemother and assistant in charge of each house. They are responsible for the general running and cleanliness of the house, and much depends on them as to whether it is a house or a home.'

Matron Longley was waiting for me in the office. She was so tall, the white cap she wore adding inches to her height. I felt a bit like the houses under the trees dwarfed to size! But the moment I set eyes on her a sentence floated through my mind – 'I am amongst you as he that serveth' – and it was a concept that was to stay with me all my years at John Grooms.

I was appointed as assistant housemother in Lilac House and arrived a couple of weeks later ready to start.

There were eight semi-detached houses, or hostels, scattered round the grounds, and all named after trees. At the top were Cedar and Acacia. Then across a wide pathway the other side of the office building were Chestnut and Hawthorn. Chestnut included girls with a disability who had grown up in the John Grooms orphanage, and had, for a short period, borne the name 'Davenport'. The gradient of the slope was steeper after

Hawthorn. Laburnum and Lilac nestled right at the bottom, their concealment added to by the orchard that straggled the sloping lawn in front of it, now a riot of blossom.

From there, climbing up from an adjacent slope, lay Sycamore and Willow. To the right of them stood a building that always reminded me of a bungalow, though it wasn't one. There were upstairs quarters for staff. The 'tacked on' sun lounge may have given this impression. It was a small restful nursing home where our ladies were sent when they were sick. It had two wards holding six beds each, and a small isolation unit. The grounds at the back were a carpet of gold when I first came. Former tenants of the site had once planted a clump of daffodils in memory of one who died. Now they had reproduced and taken over in breathtaking profusion.

I sometimes puzzled why a site for disabled folk should have been chosen where there were slopes, and discovered the reason later. Of course these were different times. No one was accepted who could not somehow climb a flight of stairs or, in general, look after themselves.

There were no lifts in the houses then. To my mind, many of these girls and women had a great deal more to cope with in comparison with all the help given to disabled people today. It was only sheer pluck and the knowledge that no firm outside would employ them as they would have to do now, plus the fact wheelchairs were not so easy to come by, that spurred them into mobility.

Down in Lilac, dwarfed even more by the massive old oak tree that flourished a few yards from the front door, I felt isolated from the world altogether. Those first weeks I felt as though somehow I had gone back in time; the war could never have made inroads in this part of the world. But it had. There had even been casualties from it. But perhaps it was just me who savoured this strange unbroken continuity of life whose peace had never been disturbed, reaching back into the previous century. However peace was hardly the word to describe that period of heart-rending deprivation and poverty when a boy had been born who was destined to change the lives of countless disabled people over the next hundred and fifty years and, indeed, for all generations after. Could he have taken a peep into the future, though, doubtless he would not have been surprised.

Thoroughly conversant with his Bible, like St. Paul he would have known that 'Love never fails.'

Chapter 1

IN THE BEGINNING

John Groom was born in 1845, not far from St. Paul's Cathedral, and two years after Dickens had published his indicting 'Christmas Carol' and was already working on 'Dombey and Son'. John had several brothers and a sister and, although brought up in a stable Christian background, was still affected by the dire poverty prevalent on his doorstep.

Clerkenwell, within sight and sound of St. Paul's, was at that time a tightly packed district of filthy slums, with little air or light. There was virtually no drainage and no pure water supply. In 1866, more than thirty per cent of London's population were quite unable to live off their income. In the first forty years of the nineteenth century, following the Industrial Revolution, the population of London had increased from one million to two and a half million. Is it to be wondered that overcrowding was a major problem, and crime and disease rife? Labour conditions were very poor and alcohol was a temporary means of escape.

Poverty may still stalk our western civilisation today, but can it compare with those hideous slums of Victorian times? Imagine it. No help from the state. No one to care. Without an income you starved and died. It was as bleak as that. Or you took to crime and immorality, living in fetid cellars, wash-houses and dark filthy garrets. Drink, the panacea, was especially useful for pouring down the throats of the terminally ill to ease their dying. Amongst stench and noise, in alleys and courts were labyrinths of hovels called 'home' that contained only a heap of rags and straw, no fire, no food in the cupboard, the cries of the new born mingling with the wail of other young children, all huddled together with dying adults. Homes – so called – where neglected children huddled in corners on bare boards, crying themselves to sleep after working the streets all day, while their vicious guardians squandered their earnings. Beatings and the other miseries these children suffered are beyond telling.

Mercifully, the social conscience of the nation was being stirred by the great reformers of those times, who sought to break the vicious circle poverty breeds; among them Dickens, Chadwick, Dr. Barnardo, John Ashley – later to become seventh Earl of Shaftesbury – and finally, but by no means least (although with his humility and deep sensitivity he would have been the first to deny it) – John Groom.

He was only ten when his father, Paul, died and, although not the eldest in the family, he was out on the streets doing his part, finding whatever work he could to help provide for them. He saw at first hand the begging, thieving and pickpocketing that went on. He knew all about the tough life of the errand boys and the street sellers. He was often cold and tired himself and shared in the experiences of the fatherless, but already compassion was stirring within him to do what he could to alleviate the suffering he saw around him every day.

From the many children he found around the markets scrounging for food, he would select a few to take back with him to his modest home for hot soup that would restore to them a little hope. His sister, Jessie, would show a great deal of ingenuity stretching resources and she and others were soon pooling their efforts to help those in desperate need, unaware of the great things that would result from these early efforts.

In 1862 John began an apprenticeship with William J. Bastard at 32 Gloucester Street, Clerkenwell, as an engine turner – the trade of ornamenting or engraving intricate and beautiful patterns on silver items such as boxes or photograph frames. Not only was he successful in completing his apprenticeship, but soon he started his own business as a metal engraver and toolmaker, a trade later carried on by his sons.

At the age of sixteen John was already teaching in Sunday School and when he was eighteen, running parallel with his apprenticeship, he was invited to share in the work of the London City Mission and began open air preaching and the teaching of the Scriptures at cottage meetings.

Soon afterwards he accepted an offer to become Superintendent of the Farringdon Mission in the City of London and that was really the beginning of his life's work. He loved preaching and conducted services in halls, streets and schools, describing himself as a voluntary evangelist of the Mission. He worked fearlessly among criminals and won their confidence and respect, paying midnight visits to their kitchens and praying with a dying burglar while his associates stood around, respectfully quiet. It was one way he could show God's love for them. He had no diplomas in social science, only the strong perception of a pioneer social reformer. In his booklet 'The Romance of John Grooms Crippleage and Flower Girls' Mission' he writes:

> 'What a childhood – a life of cruelty and despair, neither school nor play. To them the outlook only presented the prospect of becoming like the adults for whom they slaved, thus perpetuating the evil. The evil was apparent to all. Everyone knew the remedy was to remove the children from such influence, educate, inspire them with noble ideas of self-respect, of duty and true citizenship. The great question was, whose duty was it? Who would undertake the work, for its cost would be great in money, time and human strength. The vicious guardian lived upon what the children brought in and there was no thought for how money was obtained – profits or sales, alms-begging or dishonesty – there was no observance of moral law. The "widow" dodge, with hired baby or other children, was practised. The crippled child on a go-cart was a source of income to the one who had charge; such guardian resented any approach to the rescue and care of the child. "What is to become of me," says a disreputable woman, "if you take this child away?"
>
> The woman lived and was drunken through the sufferings, cries and neglected condition of the child: the child was nothing, simply a means to an end – drink.'

John saw the need in every street, but what could he do? He had little money, no premises, except perhaps the use of some rooms at his mission church, and no government aid. He was busy at his trade, too. But he cared so desperately he knew it was a mission upon which he must embark, and by God's help he would.

Did he not believe that with God all things were possible? To ask, seek and knock, and doors would open? And there was the promise of Malachi: to prove the Lord of Hosts, and see if He will not open the windows of heaven and pour out a blessing so vast there shall not be room enough to receive it. Of course he believed. Now was the time to act upon those promises and see them work out in practice, his sole aim being to raise the lives of disabled and deprived people to a fresh dignity and a new purpose and to bring them to the knowledge of the Lord he so loved.

John A. Groom
FOUNDER

Chapter 2

WATERCRESS AND FLOWER GIRLS

Not far away from the Groom home there was a vegetable market at Farringdon and the flower market at Covent Garden. When the main selling was completed there were often inferior flowers or cresses left, which were sold to children. These poor children made them into bunches and hawked them from street to street to the accompaniment of one of London's street cries – 'Cresses, fresh watercresses.' Flowers were made into posies and buttonholes and sold at stations, in the streets and around the theatres. 'Lovely sweet violets,' and 'Go on, Sir, she's a nice lady,' were all part of the selling patter.

Henry Mayhew, well known social historian of the Victorian era, quotes:

> 'One of these flower girls had come out of prison a short time previously. She was not nineteen, and had been sentenced about a twelve-month before to three months' imprisonment with hard labour, for "heaving her shoe" as she said, "at the Lord Mayor to get a comfortable lodging, for she was tired of being about the streets." After this she was locked up for breaking the lamps in the street. She alleged that her motive for this was a belief that, by committing some such act, she might be able to get into an asylum for females. She was sent out into the streets by her father and mother at the age of nine to sell flowers. Her father used to supply her with the money to buy the flowers and she would take the proceeds of the day's work home to her parents. Frequently she would be out until past midnight, and seldom or never got home before nine. She associated only with flower girls of loose character. The result may be imagined.'

Mayhew also gives an account of an eight year old who had lost all her childish ways, and knew no more of London than the part she had seen on her rounds, and thought it was all like Farringdon Market. She was pale and thin from deprivation, wrinkled where her dimples ought to have been and sighed frequently. She told him, 'I go about the streets with watercress, crying "Four bunches a penny, watercresses." I used to go to school, but I wasn't there long. I've forgot all about it now, it's

Victorian flower girls

such a long time ago.' Then she went on to portray in her own inimitable Cockney fashion what life was like for her.

She had to be down at Farringdon Market by four or five o'clock in the morning to purchase her cresses, or she didn't get any, so many were there buying earlier. It meant rising very early in the dark and cold and dressing by the light of the lamp from the court outside. Sometimes her hands were so cold it hurt to handle the cresses, which were even colder, especially when held under the pump to wash. Prices had risen from one penny per bundle to 'tuppence' (just under one penny today!). So she bought three pennyworth and tied them in as many bundles as she could, making each one look as 'puffed out' as she could, otherwise nobody would buy them. She was so unused to a good dinner she couldn't keep it down if she was given one. She had a bit of meat on Sundays, but for the rest of the week lived on two slices of bread and a cup of tea for breakfast, and this was repeated when she got home at ten o'clock for supper.

It was poor mites like these who John Groom began to invite into his Mission. They would be tempted by the prospect of hot soup and bread. The most needy were given breakfast tickets, and for dinner during the winter months, at a cost of three-farthings, plum or currant pudding made by voluntary workers from broken bread collected from the steward of a large club. Spare clothes were provided while their own ragged garments were patched and washed by a small band of willing workers. They also had to be encouraged in personal hygiene – there was no eagerness to wash hands and faces when you had never been taught to do so.

Often that repast at the Mission was their only meal of the day. Talks were given, or suitable verses of Scripture read while they were eating and, because dissolute living was so rife, temperance, thrift and self-care were prominent in the teaching. But there was still time for relaxation and games would be played. There were also Sunday services and Sunday School in Forester's Hall, in what is now Clerkenwell Road.

Through the children, John hoped the mothers and sisters in their families would be encouraged to join in these services. Even when they did, however, progress was slow in getting them to come to a new concept of themselves, of life and, what mattered most, of God. For John Groom was primarily an evangelist. He yearned for these dear souls to know themselves 'ransomed, healed, restored, forgiven,' as Henry Francis Lyte, the hymn writer, expresses it. So he told about the undeserved, unspeakable suffering and humiliation – beyond anything they themselves had endured – which the Son of God had borne to redeem them and, eventually, he began to reap a harvest.

John and his friends mustered every penny they could scrape together and, hiring a room adjacent to the Flower Market, were able to supply two slices of bread and butter and a cup of cocoa to any women and girls requiring it. Further, they provided a Club Room at Covent Garden where, each market morning, early breakfasts were served and two missionaries were in attendance to follow up cases of despair and extreme destitution. From this developed a soup kitchen, clothing club and a boots and blankets club. Again, some received more than they came for: an awareness of a God who had supplied their needs through His servants, a God Who loved them. In yielding to Him, they found their lives ennobled.

As the work continued to grow, John soon saw that there was a need to form a committee to exercise proper control. In 1865, while John was still only a very young man just emerging from his teens, a body of men and women united, with him as their leader, and the mission work began in earnest. They had no fixed centre for their work but used a number of halls. In 1866, the first service of this organisation known as the Watercress and Flower Girls Christian Mission was held. Although the saving and feeding of these children of the slums was vital work, it was soon realised that something more than the provision of breakfasts must be done to help the flower-sellers. Many of them had no real homes, and their work kept them out in the streets all hours. They endured all weathers. If it rained they had no place to dry their clothes, mud-splashed from the wheels of passing traffic. So centres were opened near markets where mid-day meals were supplied and clothing dried and repaired.

As workers increased, so did the field of activity, extending to Clerkenwell, Smithfield, Ludgate, St. Giles and the West End. It was becoming increasingly clear that a fixed base was essential, so that workers had an assembly point and the needy knew where they could come to seek help. So rooms were hired in Harp Alley, a humble spot off Farringdon Street not far from Ludgate Circus. It was the first permanent centre for the work, and what a busy place it became.

A number of well-known people gave a lot of encouragement to the workers. Among them was the great reformer, the 7th Earl of Shaftesbury. John's first meeting with

Lord Shaftesbury

Lord Shaftesbury was in Piccadilly Circus. A flower-seller there was involved in an accident. Her home-made crutch had broken and the girl had fallen into the road clutching her flowers. John was doing what he could to help her when he was summoned to a carriage that had stopped close by. The interested gentleman who had called him to enquire what was going on was the noble Lord Shaftesbury, and as a result of this incident he became one of Groom's most powerful allies. He promised to speak at the Watercress and Flower Girls first conference, and when he arrived the hall was so full that some were sitting on the stairs and those who could had climbed on to the window sills. He spoke with such understanding and sympathy that he won the confidence of his listeners immediately.

'God being our Helper, we will help you,' he concluded, 'if you will yourselves help us to help you. I will be President of your Mission.' It seemed that the cheering that broke out then would never stop, and the bond he had formed not only remained but grew stronger over the years.

He possessed influence and contacts for drawing in and providing the funds required. Among those contacts were Samuel Morley, Sir Edward Henderson (Chief Commissioner of Metropolitan Police) and Lady Henderson, F A Bevan and the Baroness Burdett-Coutts. These all took a very deep and active part in the Mission, giving their advice and enabling many new schemes to be started, but nothing they did was so far-reaching as that of Lord Shaftesbury.

Centres continued to be added as part of the main work: Bermondsey, Bloomsbury, Chelsea, Holborn, St. Luke's Whitecross Street, St. Pancras and Westminster.

Lord Shaftesbury had started a Fund that granted loans free of interest to women street hawkers in winter when flowers were scarce, for it was a principle of Lord Shaftesbury never to

Harp Alley, Clerkenwell EC1

pauperise. He gave to the sick, the helpless and bereaved, but for those capable of it, he believed in encouraging them to earn rather than be recipients of charity. It enhanced the value of every penny. And even trying to make the helpless more helpful to themselves would activate a spirit of self-reliance leading to self respect. So, in the long run, he believed they could do much better for themselves than mere charity could provide.

An example is the suffering of the flower-sellers during the prolonged and excessive frost of 1895 which was severe and brought disease and starvation. They could not get flowers for some time after the frost had gone, and each girl was given a small capital sum to enable her to restart. Meanwhile, tickets for bread, grocery and coal were widely distributed. At the Mission Headquarters during that year, 100,000 free meals were supplied in addition to those taken to the homes of the poor.

When visited by one of Groom's missionaries, a mother with young children, who was the widow of a mechanic, said that she had been five weeks without a flower to sell. She had tried her best but had been unsuccessful in getting any other work either, for her children were a handicap as well as being a great anxiety. She had sold one thing after another from her home and finally the shopkeeper could grant her no more credit: though he knew she was honest, the limit had been reached. Thinly clothed, hardly any bed covering, and no light, the little family were shivering in 20 degrees of frost and in utter despair. Had they gone to the workhouse, mother and children would have been separated and treated as paupers. It was a God-send to receive tea, food, warm blankets and provision for a fire.

The influence of Lord Shaftesbury in shaping and forming this caring organisation was, without doubt, very great and he remained President until his death in 1885. Of the floral tributes that graced his funeral, two stood out above all others to show how he was loved from the richest to the poorest. One was from the Crown Princess of Germany, the other – from 'The Flower Girls of London.'

After his death, reports tell of the continuing work: 4,000 free breakfasts each week during the winter months; 800 half-penny dinners; a total of 96,000 meals served over the year.

John Groom had plans for a long term future. Such plans included annual holidays by the sea for those he rescued, a training centre to fit them for a worthwhile job, homes, care and meaningful work for the disabled girls, and an orphanage for the

Group of 'crippled' girls (c 1906)

children who had been lost or deserted by their parents.

How all these plans were brought to realisation is to be related, but it is important to notice that as the needs changed, so did the direction of the work. Old centres were closed where no longer required, but new ones opened, ready to care in the right way, in the right place and at the right time. A flexible approach is still very much alive in the heart of the Association today.

In 1894 Forester's Hall, where their services had formerly been held, was unfortunately burnt down, and the Watercress and Flower Girls Mission services were held in Woodbridge Chapel, Woodbridge Street, instead. This site in Clerkenwell had a unique history going back to the time of the first Queen Elizabeth. Enjoying the royal patronage at the time, Thomas Sekforde was, in the year 1564, granted the Manor of Woodbridge for the sum of £764.8s.4d, an investment of land which produced a good return. In 1826, the whole estate was replanned. Impressive Georgian houses were built on the site. These were the houses which were later to become homes for John Groom's disabled workers. John lived in one of these houses – No. 8 Sekforde Street.

There appears to have been a small chapel on the Woodbridge estate and it is thought this was the site of the one re-built in 1834 that John Groom pastored. Formerly belonging to a congregation of High Calvinists of the Independent Order that had phased itself out, it had been put up for sale.

John found the premises substantial and commodious, and he and his friends earnestly sought the Lord's will in the matter of purchasing it.

A large firm of distillers had offered three times as much as John could afford. Already the large schoolroom attached to the chapel had somehow been used as a gin vault - an odd

Woodbridge Chapel, Clerkenwell EC1

29

circumstance (for some strange reason!) allowed by the Trustees. But it was quite certain they now wanted it back in Christian hands, for they unanimously and unconditionally allowed John full lease of all the premises involved for a mere £100, plus the related legal expenses (possibly for getting rid of the gin merchants!)

John Groom expounds scripture to group of blind girls

The working of Divine Providence was never more clearly seen. With possession of Woodbridge Chapel in the hands of John Groom's Mission, all debts were discharged, the building was cleaned and put in a state of good repair and, on the first Sunday in 1895, the first evangelistic service was held there.

From then on, with John as Pastor, the work of the chapel thrived remarkably. It became the heart of his evangelistic work.

At one time, as many as 500 children filled the Sunday School and 300 were present at the Band of Hope meeting. Many other children's services were held as well as Bible Classes and Christian Endeavour meetings.

John was only 21 when he began his Pastorship and it was to last for 52 years. His preaching was earnest, Bible-based, and the message urgent and simple. The sermons may have seemed long by present day standards, but not to the people of those times for

John Groom's family

they were very popular. While at Forester's Hall John had attracted a congregation of approximately 900: at Woodbridge Chapel, attendances increased still further.

Several of the Groom family were members of the 40-strong Woodbridge Brass Band. After morning and evening services they would emerge from the chapel to march round the Clerkenwell streets, often to stop in the courts and alleys and invite anyone to join in singing a popular hymn and to listen to a few very earnest words from the Woodbridge Chapel speakers.

The chapel would be filled for the monthly song services. The Brass Band would be there, the choir and the soloists. John had married Sarah Farrington, who was of great practical help to him in the women's meetings. Over the years they were to have three sons and a daughter. The eldest son, Alfred, was to become organist at the chapel. He also played a reed instrument and at these concerts would accompany the soloist. Thick red felt pads would be set out on the gallery stairs to provide extra seating and each pew had an extra pop-up seat in the gangway. With some 800 people present, the organ and a brass band the volume of sound, though happy, must have been deafening!

Another side of John's evangelistic work was to hold open air services on Clerkenwell Green during the summer months. The Green was rather like Speakers Corner at Hyde Park, a free-for-all in airing views on almost any subject – but usually of a religious or political nature. John always had a large and attentive gathering. During the summer, too, there were Sunday School outings to Clacton-on-Sea. A big display was made of these. Starting at 6.30a.m. from the Chapel and led by the Woodbridge Brass Band, the whole party would march to Liverpool Street station to board the special train to Clacton. On return, the same reception committee would be there to march them triumphantly back! It was such a great thrill for the children and their families to experience a day by the sea, presumably it had to be commemorated in some lively fashion.

Even up to the 1980s there were still many who could recall those days of lively Christian witness, and doubtless there are still some around able to do so at this time of writing.

Chapter 3

JOHN GROOM'S FAMOUS FLOWERS

The Flower Girls' Brigade had first been formed in 1878. Flower-sellers were trained and organised to take orders, make them up and deliver them for decorating dinner tables, weddings, concerts and such like. A trade by post developed and flowers were sent to many parts of the country. Each member wore an ivory badge and was instructed not to press customers to buy more flowers than ordered – a crafty trick often tried by street flower sellers.

From this developed the Flower Girls' Sisterhood. An ancient photograph reveals them as rather formidably dressed in black blouses, long black skirts, stiff white Eton collars with elegant white bows, stiff white cuffs and cuff-links. They wore a neat black hat, anchored beneath the chin with ribbon. They certainly needed to be tough, as well as compassionate, when called upon to tramp the streets in the dangerous hours of darkness in order to sort out some family problem, or work with the homeless. They did a splendid job.

But now a totally new era of caring for disabled people was destined to open up. The Flower Girls' Brigade was changing. A considerable number of school leavers were being trained for domestic service which kept them off the streets and gave them a home. Those unsuited for domestic service, and the larger proportion of these were disabled, were dressed in a neat uniform and, by permission and under the care of the police, were given stands at Hyde Park Corner, Marble Arch and other public places. Ten women were employed to purchase and prepare the flowers for sale and keep the sellers supplied. Within eleven years no less than 700 girls had been trained. But what about those whose disability did not make this the ideal solution? Those not tough enough, or whose disability unsuited them to life on the streets?

John knew the time had come for a change of plan.

Handmade flowers were becoming popular at this time. They were being imported mainly from France and Germany. John saw potential in this. No other charity was engaged in artificial flower making and it seemed symbolic that this was what he must choose for his Flower Girls to follow. The work would be light and colourful and would enable those who were disabled to use their creative skills to the full, for John planned a skilled business with skilled workers who could sell to the best markets, to wholesalers, private customers and friends at full market prices. They could use some of the rooms in Woodbridge Chapel until the work had developed sufficiently to warrant its own industrial centre.

John was also reluctantly coming to see that his mission work could no longer be continued on a voluntary basis. It was demanding too much of his time. So he finally yielded to the persuasion of his friends to leave the running of his engraving business to others and devote the whole of his time to what was to be known as 'The Industrial Training Home', though eventually to become 'John Groom's Crippleage'. He learnt how to make the flowers himself and persuaded his brothers to join him. They could work the machinery that stamped out the flower petals.

He was still living at No 8 Sekforde Street, and as houses adjacent became available he scraped together the money to rent them and provide homes for his workers. One can well imagine that, coming from the poorest homes, or from uncaring parents – even from the workhouse – being offered a good safe home, good food and a job with pay, plus a considerable measure of independence, was like being offered sheer bliss! John lived alongside his girls. He knew all of them by name, sharing their environment, their work-day, their hopes and fears, and giving them great encouragement. He was more like a father than their employer.

The seven rented houses were run by housemothers. There were twelve girls to a house. Each house had three floors, which was not ideal since there were no lifts. The more disabled girls, who couldn't mount the stairs, had to sit down and pull themselves up as best they could, or be carried up. But it was a small hardship to those who had endured so much worse, and for the late 1800s the whole scheme was a remarkable concept.

The girls were received into the home without payment and trained for two years. They were clothed, sheltered, fed, and

Flowergirls and housemother

taught to make the flowers for which they were given a wage. Out of their earnings they paid towards their board and lodging. They were not, of course, able to pay the full cost. After two years they were boarded out with foster parents and became self supporting by work being provided for them, while other girls took their places in the home. In the early days between 60 and 70 girls were in training at a time. They worked from 8 o'clock in the morning until 6 o'clock at night, which were reasonable hours for those times. After the day's work stopped (while the workroom was on Mission premises), tables were dismantled and the room prepared for the meetings of the Band of Hope, Christian Endeavour or any other club activity planned for the evening.

Time and money had had to be spent on materials and training before the work could be fully developed. Early days had been full of disappointment and weariness, meeting with failure upon failure. But steady perseverance had ultimately begun to show the work was suited to the capacity of the girls. Only the simplest flowers were made to start with, but these were good lifelike copies of natural flowers, made in cloth by hand. As the girls became experienced and settled to the work, they grew more and more ambitious. Chrysanthemums, dahlias, carnations, lilies and even orchids were made and sold to London wholesale houses, while work produced in excess became the basis of stock for exhibitions.

All the latest improvement in tools, appliances and machinery were utilised with success. The rapid progress of the

John Groom with flowergirls making flowers in Sekforde Street factory

girls was remarkable when they began to realise the possibilities. Those who did not have sufficient skill for flower work were engaged in less exacting tasks, making fancy boxes, covers for books and other items. Even girls with the use of only one hand were not debarred. Often they proved themselves well able to undertake certain parts of the work effectively.

By far the greater number of disabled people at that time were suffering from diseases of the spine, bones and joints, and almost entirely caused by tuberculosis. The next highest number were those without arms or legs, while the number of blind and partially blind and those with congenital deformities and rickets was almost as high.

Miss Last was a housemother at 38 Sekforde Street. She died aged over 100. I was privileged to know her and she often gave me 'housemotherly' advice when I first joined Grooms staff at Edgware. She tells of Corrie Wilson, who was a polio victim, and of how she used to climb the stairs at Sekforde Street on her bottom, dragging herself up each one. She had suffered eight operations on her legs, but remained unable to walk. Yet she was a most happy girl, full of fun and laughter. Miss Last had seventeen girls to look after with eight shillings a week (40p) to keep each girl. She did the shopping and the cooking, but had an assistant to do the cleaning. The girls made their own beds and helped with the washing up.

I also knew Miss Allard, who was a housemother for 53 years and died aged 99. She tells of the £5 per week she was allowed for housekeeping in those early days. She did all the washing herself to save money for food, and was proud of the fact she could always give her girls a good breakfast. They had margarine and dripping all the week with butter on Sundays.

Edna Stagg was a disabled lady I was also privileged to know. She died at the grand old age of 96. She knew John Groom personally, his daughter Maud and his three sons, Alfred, Herbert and Edward. Her father had been very strict and she had had to go to church and Sunday School every Sunday, being pushed there in a bath chair. Her father was out of work and they had come down to London from Wiltshire hoping for better things. Her sister went into service, and her two brothers left home, but her stepmother made Edna a drudge, despite the fact she was walking on unhealing fractured femurs.

Her Sunday School teacher came to the rescue and wrote to John Groom, asking if his Association would take her, and she was accepted in 1908. She went straight into the Sanatorium in Sekforde Street, and from there to University College Hospital where she had five operations on one leg. As soon as she recovered, she began work as an artificial flower maker and proudly recalled making a rose for the Queen Mother when, as Duchess of York, she visited the workrooms.

Edna could 'never say anything bad about John Grooms.' They looked after her in every way, keeping her in work and pocket money – sixpence a week, at first! But sixpence went a long way in those far off days. Later it went up to one shilling (5p) and then to five shillings (25p). On top of that, if John Groom met her or any other girls in the street, he would often give them sixpence to buy sweets for themselves.

Now that the flowers were being produced at a great rate, with true business acumen, John sought further publicity by arranging large exhibitions in Town Halls in many of the major towns of the country. This meant travel for some of the disabled workers who had to join the exhibition to demonstrate how they made the flowers and, in view of the normal confinement of their lives, they must have enjoyed this outlet immensely.

But the huge success of these exhibitions brought rather a

sting in the tail. There was a loss of financial gain because some of the subscribers thought their money was not so much needed with the success accruing from the sale of the flowers. They overlooked that the handicaps of many of Groom's workers slowed up production, and that subsidy was still required. But it was only a slight set-back. That the work continued to be blessed can be judged by the fact that in 1892 there was both a May festival and sale of work in re-built Forester's Hall. The Royal Patrons listed were HRH The Princess of Wales, HRH The Duchess of Fife, HRH The Duchess of Teck (later Queen Mary), and HRH The Princess of Hanover. Her Grace the Duchess of Westminster performed the opening ceremony. The large hall was arranged as a bower, complete with maypole and festooned with flowers. Stalls illustrated the various branches of the work.

'To the Floral Exhibition'

Using their own handmade flowers, the girls were invited to decorate the Guildhall for the Mayoral Banquet of 1906, and then a further invitation came to do the same for the banquet and reception of the King and Queen of Norway, when 30,000 blooms were used, bringing high commendation from all concerned. Flowers were also displayed at the British Industries Fair.

Obviously the need was growing to increase workroom and warehouse accommodation and, after raising the sum of £10,000 for this purpose, a fine new building was erected on a corner site

New factory opens at Sekforde Street, Clerkenwell EC1

in Sekforde Street. Here the girls could work under ideal conditions, the rooms being large, light and well ventilated with a lift between floors. Later, two further factories were built, one in Woodbridge Street and another in Haywards Place to cope with demand.

On Wednesday 26th June 1912, something very important happened. It was the very first **flag day** for collecting money for charitable causes: it was known as Alexandra Rose Day because it was instigated by Queen Alexandra, wife of Edward VII. The inspiration came from the country of her birth and upbringing, Denmark. She had the idea from a Danish priest who, seeking to raise money for the care of disabled children, sold wild roses from his garden. Alexandra adapted it for use in England, her adopted land. She was a very generous lady and the Royal household were often concerned about her giving. One official commented: 'Her generosity was unending – her income was not!' King Edward VII went further and said he was glad that the crown jewels were safely locked away in the Tower!

John Grooms was not the only beneficiary of the Flag Day, many hospitals and other institutions were, too, but every one of those roses sold on that first Flag Day was handmade from cotton by the disabled flower girls of John Grooms. Thousands and thousands of them, a pink mountain of cotton roses. Queen Alexandra had heard of the excellent work Grooms were doing in employing disabled women to make artificial flowers and honoured them by placing the first order. But it was by no means the last, for it was a commission that was to go on for 73 years, until the cost of handworking became uneconomic. Each rose, being hand made, needed some five different operations. Pink, vat dyed dressed cotton came from the manufacturers in rolls and was cut to the flat outline of the rose, using specially made cutters and a hydraulic press. The flat rose was then placed in a mould and, using heat and pressure, was given the form of a natural rose. This process was called veining. A pin was inserted, topped by a yellow centre, which secured the pin to the rose. The 'specials' used for decoration were larger, more elaborate, and called for greater skill. To a large extent printed roses are now used. Some cotton roses are produced today, but not by John Grooms.

The first Alexandra Rose Day was a day of great excitement. All over London were thousands of women strikingly dressed in white organdie and muslin with red and white sashes national colours of Denmark – selling the roses. A considerable number amongst them were titled ladies. It must have been a bright and lively contrast to the grey surroundings of the city. Even the taxis dashing to and fro throughout the day, which were used to re-stock sellers' supplies, were garlanded with roses. And it was rare to see a pedestrian not wearing one.

London taxi decorated for Alexandra Rose Day, with John Groom

Alexandra rose making in the Edgware workrooms in the 1950's

Queen Alexandra herself made a grand tour visiting the sellers and, such was her commitment to the cause, she continued this royal drive every year, even when her age and failing health was making it more of a chore.

There is another rose that figures prominently in the John Grooms records. For many years subscribers had received a red rose at Christmas. This emblem seemed a most suitable buttonhole to be worn on April 23rd, St. George's Day, and the decision was taken to promote this appeal among a cross-section of the community. Such was its success that the promotion was extended and the staff at many City banks, large businesses, the Stock Exchange and Lloyds' Underwriters were keen to wear the national emblem on April 23rd. The idea having been successfully launched in Britain, it was subsequently decided to extend it to British ambassadors and consuls throughout the world.

Only a small number of girls could make the roses but, at a time when the workrooms were short of work, these particular girls were assured of employment for many weeks of the year. Such was the importance of the rose to John Grooms – one might easily infer it was its own emblem!

Chapter 4

BETWEEN TWO
WORLD WARS

A very anxious period for the Association developed during World War I. Income decreased, while demands on resources increased. There were still flower sellers on the streets for whom John Groom felt responsible. As men from the streets and markets answered the call of their country, so did the stronger young girl street hawkers, leaving only the elderly and the very young to struggle on in the darkened streets of London, trying to sell diminished stocks at excessive prices. Queen Alexandra made her own gesture of sympathy, granting money to 200 of them in compensation for their loss of salary.

Not only had John Groom the disabled girls to consider, but 250 children in the orphanage homes he had begun at Clacton (their history to be related later). In all, he had 1,000 disabled girls, women and children to care for, with no state aid forthcoming, and the purchasing power of the pound decreased by at least 33%, compared with pre-war.

There was a shortage of food and clothing and the safety of the girls and children was a continual anxiety as German zeppelins passed over the coast to raid London and other large towns. John Groom, in his concern, was often seen going up and down Sekforde Street during air raids, in carpet slippers, and still wearing his top hat – so great was his anxiety to make sure his charges were safe!

He insisted that the utmost economy must be practised. 1916 seems to have hit an all time low. Though finances were at their lowest, demands on funds alarmingly increased. Despite expenditure being carefully controlled, practically all the income was being used, only very small sums being carried forward to start a new financial year. But John, in his seventieth year at the outbreak of war, was still a man of great faith. He had taken on

In
EVER ABIDING MEMORY
— of —
JOHN ALFRED GROOM
BORN 15TH AUGUST 1845,
DIED 27TH DECEMBER 1919,
FOUNDER OF
THE CRIPPLEAGE,
CLERKENWELL, LONDON,
AND THE ORPHANAGE
CLACTON-ON-SEA.
A SERVANT OF GOD
AND A FRIEND OF THE POOR,
THE ORPHAN
AND THE AFFLICTED.

John Groom's grave, Highgate

the work and, with God's help, he would continue undaunted by difficulties. And the work did survive the war in reasonable shape, and in a state of readiness to cope with the problems of the post war years.

That there were no casualties among those in his care as the result of enemy action was a cause of particular thanksgiving. But for John, even as the war ended, the battle was over for him, too. In his 73rd year (1918) he wrote in deep sadness to his supporters after 52 active years in the work to which God had called him:

'I am compelled to relinquish into other hands the active prosecution of the work, though my doctor holds out hope that, with rest and care, I may be spared some time yet to place my service, counsel and experience at the disposal of those who are taking up the responsibility.'

He left his house at Sekforde Street and went to live at his beloved Clacton, though he paid many visits to London and, as often as he was able, continued to take services at Woodbridge Chapel. But his health did not improve, despite the skill of the medical profession and the devoted loving care of his second wife, Ada. He died, aged 74, on 27th December 1919 and was buried at Highgate Cemetery.

The funeral service was held at Woodbridge Chapel, the chapel being crowded with people who came to give thanks for the life of this man of great faith who had believed in achieving the well-nigh impossible. Former street sellers were there; the blind, the disabled, the orphans, and representatives of the many thousands who had been helped by him. The children came, and the staff. His congregation were there, and many, many friends. It was a simple service, just as John wanted, but the vivid impression left of that service was the masses of banked flowers which filled every corner. They were not from great institutions or nobles, but from ordinary folk who had been lovingly helped by John Groom.

And perhaps this is the greatest tribute to his life.

John had chosen his successors with care, those who shared his active faith. Several years after his death those Trustees who succeeded him were going to be faced with just about the most major decision in the history of John Grooms. It would put their faith to a vital test. Leases on the workrooms were not so pressing, but the leases on the Sekforde Street houses were due to expire in 1932. There was the prospect of having to renew the leases at a much higher rental for premises which, although delightful examples of Georgian design and their tenants happy living there, were not ideally suited for disabled people.

The problem of what to do had been exercising the Council for many years. As far back as 1921 they had been deliberating whether to pay higher rents or, far better, move right out of London to purpose built dwellings and workrooms. But times were bad. The (1926) General Strike was still casting a shadow over the country, unemployment was high and the National budget for 1932 was £170 million in the red! It was not a time to be adventurous – even foolhardy to try.

But here was a case where the 'foolishness of God proved wiser than men,' for His overshadowing was still upon John Grooms, and He had other men and women lined up in the wings waiting to play their part, at a given time, in His divine plan. As so often happens when we place all our trust in Him, He simply steps over all that is negative.

Edward Cooke was Chairman at the time and he was told of an 11 acre farm 'Stoneyfields' near the then new Watford By-Pass. The farmer, old Mr. Harrington, made a modest living from a few cattle as he awaited the inevitable encroachment of houses spreading out from London. The site was for sale and would not be on the market for long; it was in too desirable a position.

One can imagine the ripple of excitement among the Trustees when Edward Cooke told them about this. There was sufficient land to build houses, a factory, nursing home, concert hall, paths, roads and gardens as well as an office block.

There was the prospect of a whole new site that could accommodate 200 disabled people in much better conditions than they were now. Transferring from London itself would prove

John Groom with his son Alfred

costly. There was a lot to think over, but while the other Trustees deliberated and prayed, one man took action.

Mr Arnold Clark, a Trustee who was also Director of a London Company and a close friend of Edward Cooke, sharing his hopes and plans for the future of John Grooms with the Council of Trustees, took a step of faith and purchased the farm privately, holding it while discussion went on. He would sell it to the Association if and when they were ready to purchase it at the price he had paid for it – his action inspired his fellow Trustees to take their personal leap of faith and meet the challenge.

Alfred Groom, who was Secretary at the time, loyally supported by Harry Blackett, was faced with the task of raising the money. Harry, a man in his sixties, had served the organisation since his teens. He was a kindly, competent man who was everyone's confidant, greatly loved and respected. Like the rest of the staff, Harry and his wife spent much time in prayer over this period. Barclays Bank, bankers to the Association since the 1880's, were outstanding in their advice and support, and subscribers gave generously. The sum of £72,000 was raised for the cost of the site and new buildings, a staggering figure for those days, and without one penny of any State aid.

So, the site paid for, building began. When finished, trees were planted and the garden laid out. Staff and residents moved in, and on 20th May 1932 the Lord Mayor of London officially opened the garden estate at Edgware Way.

But the way ahead still had to be trodden by faith. Trade was bad, but the Council never for an instant contemplated reducing the work force. Exhibitions and sales were not as successful as formerly. Money was short and halls were costly to hire. Alfred Groom tried to sell flowers to the big stores in London. It was a new experience for him to join a queue of representatives. But buyers wanted a better finish to sell in a quality market and it was therefore decided to seek new expertise in the trade. Miss Male, Miss Norris, Miss Campion and five others from Marshall and Snelgrove duly arrived and replaced Mr. Horace Thompson as Manager of the Workrooms.

The new appointment did not please the girls for they were attached to Mr. Thompson, who was married to John Groom's only daughter. So Miss Male and her team had a difficult task at the beginning, but finally won through and the quality of the flowers was improved for a higher class market. Sales were made through a wholesaler, Messrs Balfour and Company, and many

Edgware new office block

Official opening of Edgware by the Lord Mayor of London, 1932

The new Workroom at Edgware

new ideas evolved – tulips made in silk from Paris, velveteen wallflowers, orchids with the 'freckles' stamp invented by Charles Heath. Work was done to order for top fashion-houses and flowers made to match dresses. Flower capes were made for Epsom and Ascot and, as Grooms flowers began appearing more conspicuously in public shows and events, it became a source of pride and encouragement to the workers.

Another event took place in 1932. A young man of 21, known to Edward Cooke (they both attended the same church) was persuaded to join the office staff. He was Charles O'Connor, and he was to figure prominently in the future of John Grooms.

A typical case history of the type of person this new move was destined to help – how John Grooms was adapting to the times – is the story of Lorraine Hebditch, who arrived at John Grooms in the late thirties.

Lorraine had been born sound of limb, but had developed poliomyelitis at the age of nine months. Not so much was known about polio in those days. Not even the name! It was referred to as 'Infantile Paralysis'. By the time the medical profession had diagnosed the nature of her complaint, the damage was already done. Lorraine was quadruplegic. Through the skill and care of the London Hospital, Whitechapel – now the Royal London Hospital – she was given back the use of her arms, but left with a scoliosis

49

of the spine which was the major reason why she could not walk.

At that time too, disabled children were not accepted in an ordinary state school, thus she would have received no education at all if her parents had not decided it would be best for her to be sent away to the Heritage Craft Schools at Chailey in Sussex, where she would he taught to do something creative with her hands and also receive the rudiments of an education.

Rules there were very strict measured against today's standards for disabled children, but she has no regrets, for they taught her not only to walk on crutches (with callipers on her legs), but also a dogged and sturdy independence.

But back home at the age of sixteen, there was no work for her and no state aid. She was one of a large family of children, and the need to support herself was desperate. There was no obligation then, as there is now, for firms to employ disabled people. Lorraine's many failed attempts to get a job convinced her that, in those days, disabled people were looked upon as a race apart. The final humiliation was the day she went after a position and did not even get past the threshold. She was merely looked up and down by the woman who opened the door to her and told in no uncertain terms they 'did not employ people like her'!

She was thankful to have the diversion of going to toy making classes on Friday afternoons. These classes were organised by the Toc H, an organisation for Christian social service, which derived its name from the army signalling abbreviation for Talbot House, a soldiers' club founded in Poperinghe in the Ypres Salient by the Rev. (Tubby) Clayton in 1915, and named after Reginald Talbot, a young officer killed in the early days of World War I. And it was Toc H that arranged an interview for her at John Grooms, where she was told about the work, given a medical, and assured they would be writing to her.

Everything looked hopeful, yet she felt sad she would be leaving home again – though she was free to return at weekends. But when the letter from Mr. Cooke came, it was much more than a confirmation she had the job. He wrote that he would be 'very happy to welcome her into his family.' With such a nice way of putting it, she did not feel so badly about leaving her own.

She describes Edward Cooke, who had now become Superintendent, as a tall man having a rosy, Father Christmassy type of face which was always ready to wreathe in smiles. Then one day he sent for her and, since her trial period was just coming to an end, she feared dismissal. Instead, it was to praise her for her

Lorraine Hebditch

progress and express the hope she was going to remain 'one of the family' – and she was offered a sixpence-a-week rise. Then he sat back, eyed her in a fatherly way and said: 'It has been brought to my knowledge you have only one coat, Lorraine.' She wondered how he knew, and suspected he had seen her wandering about the estate during the weekends she did not go home in the same hand-me-down brown hounds-tooth coat he had seen her wearing all the week. He then went on to say he was going to get her housemother to take her to buy a new one. He would loan the money and she could pay him back sixpence a week.

For Lorraine it was like being offered a fortune! A rise, and a new coat! She couldn't remember the time she had ever had a new one! So what did it matter if the rise was going to pay for the coat! In any case, not so many weeks after she became the proud owner of a new coat, Mr. Cooke sent for her and told her she need not pay back any more money. Presumably the token gesture had been enough to make her feel she was not accepting charity. That was the kind of father figure Mr. Cooke was: a man running a real home – not an institution.

Life for disabled people in those days could prove so terribly expensive with no government help whatsoever. New boots were a problem to buy. So also were new callipers and any other surgical appliances needed. There was only one way round the difficulty. The surgeon would assess the person for whatever it was they were requiring and, without the money to buy the item for themselves, they could go off to the almoner's office to collect a book full of addresses of people who donated to various hospitals. Then it was up to the person to pick out the names they would write to, as many as were likely to cover that particular need. Each answer received was worth five shillings. Princess Alice was on

Lorraine's list. She received many a letter back from her with an accompanying note from her secretary saying, that if she needed any more help she wasn't to hesitate to ask. And kind though this charity was, it is easy to see why Mr. Cooke's generous actions made him so special.

Then came World War II, and it was again a very difficult time for the Association. Yet, in view of the uneasy situation developing in Europe, the Council of Trustees had been thinking ahead as far back as 1938, planning the possibility of needing Air Raid precautions, fire fighting, shelters, and change of work for the girls. They had so many in their care for whom they were responsible, the children and the disabled women and girls both at Edgware and still with some connection at Clerkenwell.

Once war was declared, Air Raid shelters were put up with great speed, lawns and gardens making way for them. Shelters were meant to be put underground, but Grooms had special

Digging for Victory, Edgware estate, 1942

designs drawn for easy level approach, no steps, gentle slopes and no hindrances to slow moving people – the first shelters for disabled people and another first for Grooms! Staff and girls were trained. Air Raid practices were arranged, and after the first mad scrambles, a good routine was worked out. The whole Groom's 'family' at Edgware helped in the 'Dig for Victory' campaign and the head gardener, Mr. Reeve, and his staff were able to provide enough vegetables to make the Edgware estate almost self-supporting. In view of some disabilities, testing the gas masks when they arrived proved a time of amusement, taking all the seriousness out of the situation. Part of the estate became a centre for an Air Raid Precaution station and there was training in the use of the stirrup pump to put out incendiary bombs.

Because there was a shortage of materials and the Board of Trade would not license the supply of pins for the Alexandra Roses, there was a fall in sales income, a matter which worried the Trustees.

Indeed the flower trade almost stopped. The girls now turned their finger skills to making and assembling hand microphones for military purposes, condensers and millions of desperately needed rivets. It must have been a very satisfactory thought that those rivets were going into the Spitfires which did so much valiant work in the Battle of Britain.

There were many near misses at Edgware. A German shell went through the clock tower above the offices. Despite repairs it never really kept good time again until a new electrical mechanism was installed. There was a direct hit on one of Grooms houses in Upcroft Avenue. This house was home for six disabled workers who lived off the estate. Four of them were killed outright, the other two injured and taken to hospital. It was a time of great sadness which Lorraine herself remembers. Lorraine had gone home at the outset of the war because her parents had thought it safer. But things grew financially tough for them with other little ones to care for, so she went back to Edgware. At night when the siren sounded, the bombers were often overhead before callipers, boots or shoes that needed lacing, were put on – and you couldn't walk without them. Neither could you run on crutches – though Lorraine got the nearest to it! The assistant in Lilac, where Lorraine lived, found her own solution. She would rush to the piano to thump out 'Onward Christian Soldiers' while the girls scrambled as best they could beneath the heavy dining room tables, giggling their heads off!

They had their own fire fighter, too, one of the more able-bodied girls trained to work the stirrup pump should it be needed. But she was a lass who enjoyed going out for a social evening and slept soundly on her return – then it was such a job to wake her, that by the time she got moving and into her siren suit, the raid would be over!

Once, the member of an aircraft crew baled out and his parachute brought him down on rough ground behind the house where the manageress lived. Because his leather flying jacket had the name 'Fitz' on the back, the poor man had a job proving to the disabled girls and local people who crowded around him that he was in the RAF!

The Trustees needed to keep level heads during those difficult war years. But every meeting was opened and closed with prayer, thus trusting and seeking the wisdom and guidance of God in all they did. Despite running through the war years on overdrafts kindly arranged by Barclays' Bank, which at one point went up to £25,000, they had thoughts and talks about a pension scheme for staff. They also set up an All Ladies Committee which had delegated power to take action between Trustees' meetings on certain matters. They authorised the abandoning of the pink slips scheme which every resident needed if wanting to stay out late; this gave the girls more freedom to come and go merely on signing a book so staff would know they were out.

And what of Grooms management personnel during this war-time period? In 1944 Charles O'Connor was welcomed back to the office after being seriously wounded at Salerno, in Italy. Ada Groom, second wife of John died, and Woodbridge Chapel was leased to Islington Medical Mission who took over the running of the services.

Then in 1945 as the war came to an end, the Trustees dealt with the de-requisitioning of all the premises and war damage claims. Thankfully, Grooms had come through the war in reasonable shape, set for a steady course ahead.

Not long after, I came to Grooms myself to spend many happy fulfilling years.

Chapter 5

A HOUSE – OR A HOME!

Details of what I could expect in my life at John Grooms had been aptly given to me by the introductory letter Miss Longley, the Matron, had written to me prior to my going there:

'The girls are at work from 8 until 12.30 in the mornings, and 1.30 until 5.30 in the afternoons. Breakfast and High Tea are prepared in the houses, but the mid-day meal, except at weekends, is cooked in the main kitchen and taken round to the houses.

Staff have some free time every afternoon and evening, a half day during the week and half day on Sundays, either morning or afternoon, and one day off a month.

The salary at present is £2 a week to commence, rising to £2. 5 shillings after one year's service. Three weeks holiday with pay are given each year. A uniform allowance of £3 is made in two six monthly instalments, but no set uniform is worn.

There is a superannuation scheme in force, which all employees under 50 years of age are expected to join. As it is only possible to enter the scheme in January of each year, entrance would more or less coincide with increase of salary. The employees' contribution to the scheme is two shillings per week.

We have a staff prayer meeting on Friday afternoons. Devotional services are held on Thursday and Sunday evenings open to all who care to attend.

We are very anxious that these girls should accept Christ as their Saviour, and we have a nucleus of such. So much does depend upon the staff, and very particularly on the witness of their daily lives.'

Terms of employment were stringent – even for those times but, caught up in the same sense of mission that had inspired its founder, little else mattered. I hadn't forgotten the other main objective I had been given, to make a home out of a house, and set about doing it.

A boiler fuelled by coke in the cellar below the two houses supplied the central heating, and this was regularly stoked by a caretaker. But there was still a coal fire in the dining room-cum-lounge, and my duty first thing in the morning was to see it was laid ready to be lit in the late afternoon, or straightaway if cold

Willow House in the Spring (next door to Lilac)

enough, and for a beginning what could have been more cosy and homemaking than that!

I helped with the breakfast. Then after the girls had left for the pleasant, light filled, spacious factory on the estate where the artificial flowers were made, I would trundle upstairs with my dusters, brooms and brushes and electric polisher, a bit bewildered sometimes where to start.

I found it was best to begin in the bathroom, then work my way round the cubicles. The bathroom contained two baths, two toilets, and eight washbasins. The washbasins stood four facing each other in the centre of the room. There was no privacy. A pulley hung over the basins and this was where the girls could hang their washing to dry. Each had a special time for doing this so that they did not clash with each other.

The cubicles were situated in one long corridor and two short, forming a T shape. My impression of them was of rather nice 'horse boxes'. Three sides were panelled, with a space beneath at floor level and a much wider space open to the ceiling.

So the 'girls' – as they were always referred to at whatever age – were really only partitioned off from each other. There was a window in each cubicle, and a curtain in place of a door. A bed was affixed to one side of the partition. The rest of the furniture comprised an oblong box of a wardrobe (commonly known as a 'coffin' amongst the girls!) and a small chest of drawers. In the few slightly larger cubicles there was a bed either side separated by an even smaller chest of drawers to be shared by the two occupants. Over each bed a small hanging wardrobe was fixed. It could only hold about four items of clothing. The rest had to he packed away in suitcases stowed away in the large luggage rack at the end of one of the short corridors. Over the years I was there, there were fewer girls in the houses so most of the double cubicles were allotted as singles to those who had been in the house the longest.

I mention all this because, although to our modern age it sounds like deprivation, it did not appear at all like that at the time. Instead it was the background to an atmosphere all its own, on the whole a friendly and contented one. I cannot emphasise enough the kind of underlying warmth that surrounded all my days at John Grooms. Considering the fact that we all lived and worked together, girls included, we got on remarkably well. It may have affected them in some other way, but during all my time there I have no recollection of any disabled person showing resentment of their disability.

Back downstairs I had to lay up the tables for the lunch. There were four tables with approximately six girls at each table. Then when they came in from the factory I had to help serve this mid-day meal. If it was not our turn for the daily help we shared with next door, I had to start on the washing up. The mid-day meal sent in from the communal kitchen did not always suit jaded appetites. But high tea, cooked by the housemother, or the assistant when it was the housemother's half day, was much better received.

I laid the tables for tea, but there was a rota for two girls to help me wash up afterwards and lay the tables for breakfast the following morning. Very often they would settle between them for one to help wash up while the other laid tables. And this brought me into my first vital contact with Lorraine. Walking only on callipers, she contrived a marvellous balancing act of getting around indoors without the aid of her crutches. Of an orderly mind, she had the cutlery all neatly laid out on the trolley for transferring to the tables. However, when her balance was suddenly lost, knives, forks and spoons shot up into the air like a firework display, clattering to the floor in ear splitting din. She was as floppy as a rag doll trying to get her back on her feet, but unhurt and treating it all as a huge joke.

Our modern society might consider the kitchen only one step removed from Victorian archives, but I thought it a pleasant, homely place. On one wall was a large dresser over an equally large green topped work table. A large black gas stove, sporting years of maturity, stood adjacent to it. The window overlooked

Main kitchen – preparing lunch

the orchard, for as I mentioned in the prologue, Lilac and Laburnum nestled in a dell at the lowest part of the orchard. The lilac and laburnum trees from which the houses took their names were both in fragrant blossom as I began my service at Grooms.

The kitchen sink was under the window, a large pantry to the side of it and next to that a coal cupboard; no fridge as far as I can remember. There were red tiled windowsills and polished parquet flooring. In fact the whole of the house, upstairs and down, had polished floors. Even the red stone bathroom floor was kept shiny with a non-slip polish. I understand it helped rather than hindered walking for disabled people.

On my first evening I was intrigued by the slate propped up on the work top table with names like Hetty, Ruby, Sally, Lal (short for Harriet) chalked on it. Another board also held a list of names. One recorded whose turn it was for ironing that evening, the other list was for those on late pass. All residents had to be in by 10pm, whilst 10.30pm was a late pass. These were the winter times; during the summer a half hour was added on. For those under 21, half an hour was deducted.

The housemother and I had alternate evenings off. Whoever was on duty heated the supper drinks and locked up. I cannot recall ever having to report anyone for being excessively late although to a few minutes' lapse we turned a blind eye. Quite a few residents had homes to go to at weekends. There were no restrictions other than to be in on time. Neither did the staff have to wear uniform. At one time the housemother had worn brown and cream, while the assistant wore a dress of navy blue and white, but not so now.

I was interested that some of the girls still quaintly paid into a 'penny bank'. This was a saving scheme towards clothing or anything else that might be needed. One of the girls would collect and enter this money in a book before handing it over to Mrs Cooke, who was still alive, though sadly by my time Mr. Cooke

Going home (on the workroom steps)

had died. Mr. Parker, a different personality but a caring man, had taken his place. The 'penny bank' was mentioned as far back as the time of Lord Shaftesbury when he had formed the Loan Fund, or more precisely the Emily Loan Fund, in memory of his wife. He created the Penny Bank 'to encourage thrift'.

Evening at home – in front of the fire at Lilac

A report during those Victorian times mentions both:

'A young widow, left with four children, who had the greatest difficulty to support them, found it to be needful in the winter to seek a fresh sphere of labour. Help was granted her from the Fund, with which she not only supported her family but found herself able to save her earnings, that when some few months afterwards one of her children died she drew her savings out of our Penny Bank, amounting to £1.17s.0d.'

I had been in Lilac almost a year, and was busy cleaning the cubicles one morning, when I heard the unmistakable tread of Matron Longley on the stairs. She came to tell me I would be getting my five shilling (25p) rise in salary, but only half of it would be mine! The other half would be deducted for superanuation which I would now need to start paying. Nonetheless, I felt as delighted as Lorraine had done over her sixpenny rise!

Every Friday afternoon we took it in turns to hold a staff prayer meeting in one of the houses. The only compulsory thing about it was the use of the house – attendance wasn't, though there were usually a goodly number present. A member of the staff would give a short message, then there would be a time of open prayer. Mr. Parker and Matron seldom missed attending, even if it sometimes meant, especially for Mr. Parker, putting in a late appearance.

After the pleasant news, on the morning Matron told me of my increase in salary, came the shock. Would I, she asked, lead the prayer meeting the following Friday. I still have a copy of the message I gave. I could never have 'thought' it up myself. Launching into the deep for the first time must have encouraged others. I remember one lady on the staff saying how she had been about to refuse when pulled up sharp by the thought: 'Fancy being a Christian, and not able to say a word for the Lord when asked!' Another housemother took a more humorous approach. She hadn't wanted to speak, but opening her bible for guidance her eyes fell on words in Deuteronomy – 'be not afraid of their faces!'

The girls were always the centre of our praying. In my mind there stands out one particular incident. Rose was a gentle natured person in her mid-forties. She was paralysed in one arm and lame in one leg. She suffered a bout of ill health and became very poorly. We prayed for her healing but she only grew worse. After some investigation it was decided she should have an operation. Rose put off having it because she was afraid, but after some struggle agreed to it, and was completely at peace the day she went into hospital.

Then, just as she was being prepared for the theatre, the doctors suddenly changed their minds and said she no longer needed the operation. There was no small indignation amongst us all that she should have been put through such a trauma. Rose, in particular, after having had to struggle to accept the situation, now had to change her mind.

Sharing the indignity of it all with Matron, I stopped, as a new aspect to the situation arrowed into my head. Hadn't we been praying that what was best for Rose would happen? I could see the same inner awareness of how we limit the scope of answers to our prayers was getting through to Matron. Rose, too, was to lose her annoyance under a widening vision. When she died a few years later, it was from entirely different causes than those that had sent her into hospital in this instance.

We still had Sekforde Street girls in the houses and we learnt a lot about the old days from them. Elizabeth Price – or 'Lizzie' as we all knew her – told how once it had been compulsory to go to church on Sundays. Those who didn't want to go found a way out – or thought they had! They would dress in their Sunday best as though intending to go, then creep back up to their sleeping quarters and hide under the beds until they knew the housemother had gone. Except for one occasion when she proved as wily as they were. She banged the door shut as though she had left, then tip-toed back up the stairs.

'You can all come out,' she admonished blandly. 'I know you're there!'

Sheepishly they crawled out, and in the tradition of the Pied Piper of Hamelin, followed where she led them!

Church-going was no longer compulsory now, though Mr. Cooke, in his time, had expressed a wish for the girls to attend a service at least once on Sundays. He and Mrs. Cooke had held an informal weekday gathering in their bungalow 'Kafue', close to the Stoneyfields Lane entrance, and it was open to all. After Mr. Cooke died, Mrs. Cooke continued with these meetings. They were the highlight of the week for many. By the time I came to Grooms, these meetings were coming to an end. Frail from advancing years, Mrs. Cooke could no longer continue with them. The homely warmth and peace they engendered somehow seemed lost for a while when the new building known as the 'Quiet Room' was built opposite Chestnut and the meetings were transferred there. They gained momentum after a while, though, and attendances grew, more than could have been accommodated in the bungalow. They followed the format of hymns, prayer, choruses and a message. Mrs. Stroud, housemother of Chestnut, was our pianist and was also responsible for booking a different speaker each week.

Every Sunday evening there was a service in the Quiet Room led by a dedicated team from Woodcroft Hall at Burnt Oak. It had its regular attenders who could not get out to church, and the staff were glad of it, too, if they happened to be on duty. Regularly they gave us a New Year party in our concert hall. Sir John Laing, the builder, was associated with this Christian community – though this was the era before he was knighted – and we at Grooms were the recipients of many kind and generous gestures from him and his wife.

For a while the church of John Keeble at Mill Hill arranged an early morning monthly Communion Service in the Quiet Room for any girls or staff who cared to attend, regardless of the denomination we belonged to. Those of us who made the effort to be there just after six, found early rising a small price to pay for the enrichment it gave our day.

So between the years 1950 – 1965, I can personally testify that the evangelistic fervour of its founder was very much alive at Grooms. Each house was a home and somehow reflected individual characteristics of its own under the influence of its Christian staff: homely Miss Allard of Willow, who was to be a housemother for 53 years, a real 'Mum' who openly professed it as her home as well as the girls. Then there was gentle Miss Last of Roseway, where to enter was to encounter an aura of peace; also Eileen Seller, housemother of Sycamore, who turned her house into a home with flowers and bric-a-brac. She had a free ranging budgie who delighted in nipping the heads off the flowers, and, flying free one day, was rescued and returned from many miles, simply because he had been able to give voice to the fact that he lived at 'John Grooms!' Other houses in similar fashion reflected home, and the sense of vocation amongst staff bound us together as a community in a way the secular could never have done.

Chapter 6

MEMORIES OF A HOUSEMOTHER

I was nearing the end of my days as an assistant. And as it had been Spring when I started in Lilac, so it was Spring when I made the change. When may trees and the horse chestnuts were budding, and aspects of the estate were beginning to resemble a forest glade even to bluebells, and the squirrels sporting from tree to tree and cheekily climbing the walls of the factory to peer in at the window, I moved from the furthest house at the bottom of the slope to the furthest house at the top – Acacia. Outside the front door was a row of lush poplars, breathtakingly tall, and the hardy acacia tree, when it was laden with leaf and blossom, dipped down like a willow.

To prove the success of Lilac being a home rather than a house for me, the first weeks I was away from it I was terribly 'homesick'. To make matters worse, I was following in the footsteps of a well loved 'Mum' who was retiring, and I quaked at the thought of having to step into her shoes. It was Miss Waterman – the same person who, as assistant in Lilac during the war years, had thumped out 'Onward Christian Soldiers' on the piano during the air raids. I could have done with that kind of inspiration myself during those first days.

I was in my early thirties and, as far as I can remember, the youngest housemother on the estate, but six of these girls were under twenty-one, so at least it struck some balance rather than caring for all older women.

But the younger ones were the worst for testing you. You could make all sorts of blunders and be treated with tolerance, but not if you couldn't cook! I was tackling my first dinner. The living-room had two doors. One led directly into the entrance hall, the other into the kitchen. It was the weekend, so all those who had stayed indoors – and that seemed to be everyone – kept

65

Dining room – relaxing after lunch

casually walking in and out of the kitchen under some pretext or other, but to my jittery mind obviously keeping track of my progress. Free access to the kitchen was part of making a 'house' a 'home'. For once I wished it wasn't!

Mr. Reeves, the gardener, had supplied some lovely large apples, so I decided the best thing for dessert would be to bake them. Simple, too! Those seventeen rosy apples looked a picture all set out on a nice white baking tray.

I am very sorry to say the gas oven was a horrible old relic from a past age. There was no heating gauge. The mystery was how it had stood up to all those years of endless use. All the screws were loose and fell out at the least provocation. But I consoled myself that nothing could possibly go wrong with so simple a task as baking an apple. So I popped the tray into the oven and got on with washing up the pots and pans.

The smell of baking apple was pleasant. Nothing seemed wrong until I happened to turn round from the sink. Then I thought something had gone wrong with my vision. Coming out of every crevice of the oven, just like lava flowing from a volcano, and creeping insidiously across the floor to my very feet, was a molten stream of apple. You would have to have seen it to believe what it was like! For one nightmarish moment I felt I was being engulfed by it.

It was a mercy I had passed muster by then, and everybody had cleared off. I collected my scattered wits and sending up a short sharp prayer that nobody would come in, for seeing this horrifying spectacle I knew my reputation as a housemother would be at an end before it had even begun. I opened the oven door and, with gooey apple everywhere, slapped all I could rescue into a pie dish, threw in a few raisins and served it up as it was and never have I received such high praise for an improvised dish. There was hardly enough for second helpings!

My next fiasco was trying to make meringues for four o'clock tea at another weekend. I'd never attempted them before, so, wanting a bit of privacy in which to make my mistakes, I chose a particularly quiet period. I surveyed the finished product with pride. Seventeen luscious, large, pink, mouth-watering specimens ready to produce as a lovely surprise for tea on the morrow.

The assistant had a bed-sitter, while I had a bedroom and a small sitting room of my own. It was only a short distance to my quarters so I first peered round the kitchen door and, seeing no one, made a dash for it. But unfortunately there was someone about. Sharp-eyed Joan, one of the younger girls, a petite young lady whose disability was a weak spine and who, I was to discover, was herself a good cook. Thinking she had got a quick glimpse under the cloth covering them, I managed to give her the impression they were for my private consumption, but she must have thought me greedy if she believed it!

Oddly enough, I forgot all about them until we were about to sit down to tea next day. Then I remembered, dashed off to fetch them, whipped off the cover, and to my complete astonishment found myself gazing down at seventeen pink blobs! My lovely meringues had sunk to the size and consistency of a small toffee each. How glad I was I hadn't told anybody! As I sat down to tea, still bemused, trying to work out what had really happened, even wondering whether a trick had been played on me, Joan did remark she thought we were going to have meringues for tea. I replied I thought she must have had a dream. I certainly felt as though I had!

My girls, to me, were not just girls. They were each a Character, with a capital C.

To mention a few, there was nice looking Rosina, under twenty-one, lively and alert, who preferred an H.P. sauce sandwich to a good meal, and who went into the factory after lunch one afternoon to emphatically declare, against all opposition, she had been offered, not non-alcoholic (it was Ribena!) but a glass of 'apostolic' wine with her meal! Young Violet who had a lovely voice and sang in the choir. Genteel Rose, one of the older girls, and Ethel, one of the Sekforde Street ladies, who deserves a volume on her own.

Buttons was an extremely small young lady, not much more than two and a half feet tall, hence the name she was always known by, and of which she herself approved rather than her more refined Christian name of Muriel. Her great loves in the food line were Marmite and chocolate pudding. It was an enormous treat for her when we had chocolate sponge pudding for dinner. From behind a great mound, slowly and delicately masticated, would emerge Buttons. Left overs were sliced up, put back (cold) on the table for tea, and she would again work her way steadily through two or three slices. It was just as well she did; one did not expect her to eat the same as someone twice or three times her size, but one expected her to eat. If she took it into her head to do so, she could go all day without food, no amount of bullying or coaxing could make an impression.

'Eat your egg,' I was always saying.

Up would go her small nose. 'Don't like eggs. Somebody else can have it.'

There was great excitement when Dad – a fine man in the C.I.D. – or a friend, came to take her out for a meal. She came back enthusing extravagantly over the wonderful food she'd eaten.

'What did you have?' we'd ask.

'Egg and chips,' was the reply. One can only surmise that the pleasure of the excursion added a subtle flavour to the egg!

She was also a Ranger in the Girl Guides. Every so often it was field day, and off she would go, her diminutive figure smart in her uniform. First I would be approached about a week before the event to get her tin mug and plate out of storage so she could get them cleaned up. She would give them a critical examination for any traces of dust. I had to supply the knife, fork, and spoon and a raw potato. Presumably their Captain supplied the sausages.

She would come back that night full of it, having dropped the sausage she was trying to barbecue into the fire. Someone had rescued it. She had eaten and enjoyed it, and I couldn't help wishing the glamour of the camp fire had been behind all her meals.

No lover of work, she would decide on occasions a day in bed would do her a power of good. My first intimation would be one of the girls coming to tell me Buttons wasn't getting up. They knew her as well as I did and were past asking her what was wrong. The diminutive figure in the bed wouldn't move when I walked into the cubicle and banging and shaking made no impression whatsoever.

Eventually one eye would open in an extremely penetrating wide awake stare. 'When I went to get up this morning, the floor came to meet me,' was her excuse.

'Very obliging of it!' But sarcasm was completely lost on our young friend. Being so tiny, she had to be given the benefit of the doubt. It would be reported to the nursing staff, who were usually of the same opinion as me. When Buttons really ailed, she looked different, and bore her illness like a Spartan.

Usually the morning after she would saunter down, looking very bored with life, spend some time staring about her when everyone else had gone to work, then finally decide she had better follow.

I knew she was getting into trouble for being late, and once tried to chivvy her up by asking how she thought everyone would get on if I behaved like she did every morning, not bothering to get up.

She looked me straight in the eye, and without any hesitation answered:

'That's all right. We'd all have a good excuse for being late!' Only a slight gleam behind her spectacles betrayed any sign that she thought what she had said was funny. She was often involved in arguments which, in my opinion, she did not start. But she had the undoubted gift of winning them. If she had no suitable answer – which was rare – she would leave people raving to the air, using her deafness as a pretext.

Little in stature she might have been, but not in mind. Neither was she lacking in physical and moral courage. She was as wise as the proverbial owl, not merely having character. She was a Character, and I feel privileged to have known her.

Being houseproud turns a home into a prison, but neither does it make for home if everything is in an untidy muddle. During my first days in Acacia, I knew I had to get to grips with this problem somehow. In no way did I believe my predecessor had allowed coats to be flung down on settees and permanently left there, stone hot water bottles to line the kitchen sills like soldiers, waiting for their after-supper fill-up, or table cloths lazily left on the tables at weekends to save relaying. It was a 'try on' and, after a battle, some law and order was restored.

The chief offender was another Character – Doris! Nobody could ever – or would ever – compare with this inimitable Yorkshire lass. She wore one high boot and there was a weakness in her spine, but she was delicately proportioned and could have looked a gem dressed properly. Wiser and more expert people than myself had tried to change her, but to no avail. Doris still preferred to dress in three tiers. First came her dress reaching almost to her ankles, then, a couple of inches shorter, her working overall. Topping the lot, normal length at last, was her coat. Sometimes the clean but much worn cardigan she had on, shrunk from many a wash, clung round her neck as though loth to trespass any further. Never did she think of pulling down a rucked garment to its normal place. Yet she had so many clothes there was nowhere to put them all. When the dressing table groaned under bulging drawer and the wardrobe sagged from the pressure of crammed in items, Miss Delves (my assistant) and I knew we had to 'go to war'.

We took it in turns to do this. It wasn't exactly a chore. It was an entertainment. It was a job to pin our victim down to set a time for a clearance, but when at last we did, she was most affable. Her wardrobe seemed to consist of a motley collection that she labelled 'first', 'second' and 'third' best. A bewildering medley of old photographs would be thrust into our hands to distract us from the main task, but inch by inch would come the surrender. First a weary looking garment would be pressed into our hands like a consolation prize. 'You can have this, if you like.' Then by the end of the evening, cheerfully patient with us when ours was exhausted, a substantial pile (looking as though it had just come from them!) would be handed over 'for the refugees.'

One hot August bank holiday when we had been attempting one of these forays, we gave up half way because we were all a bit overcome by the heat.

I had just gone into my sitting room and was putting my feet up with a sigh of relief when there was an ear splitting explosion, followed by running footsteps and raised voices. I rushed out in great alarm and saw Doris' white night gowned figure – she had put herself to bed for the afternoon – standing at the top of the stairs, a small pile of something white lodged neatly on top of her head. She stood there, the very replica of a penitent in sackcloth and ashes, one finger pointing dramatically upwards and babbling on about the roof coming down.

Well – the ceiling had! A burst pipe had been silently leaking

'Girls' in the Quiet Room on 'library night'

away in the attic, and the pressure of water had brought down the whole ceiling above her cubicle, achieving in a few seconds what we hadn't been able to achieve for months. Huge lumps of wet concrete and plaster had targeted on half open drawers and liberally smashed down in destruction on the accumulated garments that shared the bed with Doris. The miracle was that she had escaped in such split second timing. Truly Divine Providence had saved her from what could have been fatal.

Behind her eccentric ways was a kind heart. And this is what endeared me to Doris, forced upon you though those kind deeds often were. When it was the assistant's half day off and she knew I would have to lay the tables for tea, I have known her rush to help by laying the cutlery round while others were still trying to eat their dinner, causing no end of an uproar and confusion. Opposition only met with a defiant jut of the chin, the ominous beginning of an unstoppable rush of temper. She was best ignored until she had simmered down, for Doris was a bit like the month of March. If she came in like a lion, she would go out like a lamb. It could be the other way round as well.

Another member of the Acacia family worth mentioning is Sooty, the cat – another Character with a capital C! If it is true cats have nine lives, Sooty truly tried using them up. It was Rosina

71

who had first wanted a cat, and she was soon backed up by the others. Progress in his mother's body was carefully monitored until he came into the world. There was great excitement when he was born, and even greater excitement when the tiny black scrap of fur was brought to us one golden summer evening. He was well named because I was always dragging him down from a mountaineering expedition of the flues just in time to stop him being incinerated.

His next escapade was to tightrope walk the landing banister, lose his footing and crash spread-eagled at my feet, a hissing bundle of fur. He seemed dazed for a while, but no bones were broken.

Another time there was a clatter of falling, garden tools, which were kept in the front part of the coal cupboard, plus that frightful hissing noise Sooty always gave when he was in trouble, this time prolonged. I rushed to the cupboard, and to my horror there was Sooty, upside down and with his head securely stuck between the twisted prongs of an old gardening fork.

I gathered up cat and fork, terrified he was going to strangle before my assistant and I, after a great deal of difficulty, could manage to squeeze and pull him through. He recovered before we did. Times out of number he was marooned up trees and it wasn't a case of dogs not liking cats. It was nothing to see a yelping member of the canine breed, who had dared intrude into the grounds, racing for the entrance with a small, hissing bundle of fury behind him.

On one occasion we discovered the occupant of a nearby bungalow was feeding a 'poor stray cat.' Our Sooty had found his own cunning way of getting two dinners! The elderly gentleman must have been suffering from poor eyesight. I can think of no other possible reason our pudding of a cat should have been mistaken for a starving stray!

One day we heard we would have to move out of Acacia while alterations and redecorations were in progress. Of course it included all the other houses, but we were first on the list. Despite the exhaustion of packing things away in Acacia, I rather enjoyed it. There were possession accumulators apart from Doris, and it was an impetus towards a good clearance. The more seriously disabled people moved to the other top houses, or the nursing home. The eight remaining girls, Miss Delves and myself, moved over to the vacant bungalow, 'Bolobo'. The quaintness of its name had evolved from the Boys Life Brigade, who had used the building in the early days before Grooms took over the estate.

Saturday morning revealed a pathetic procession trudging along with bundles which somehow had not found a place on the electric trolley conveying the bulk of our luggage, Sooty leading.

It was an old house, very badly in need of repair and redecorating, but I loved it. In the same way as some of my Acacia family possessed Character with a capital C, so this house bore its own personal charm for me; and since the majority of the girls were only young, they revelled in the change, deriving great fun from their communal dormitory, a large, low ceilinged room with crumbling, badly stained walls.

Glenys was on the plump side, and I made the mistake of allotting her a rather narrow bed, and a high one. When, gasping and panting, and with an obliging hoist by a couple of her neighbours she reached the summit, she promptly rolled off the other side, to the hysterical laughter of the lookers-on! I was about to get her to change with one of the other girls when she promptly went down with flu' and spent the rest of her time in the Nursing Home. An epidemic broke out, so I lost some of my flock, but I was not long left short tenanted before I began absorbing the draft from the next house so preparations could begin there.

The dining room ran the full length of the building; it was dark, but in a cosy sort of way with the wide verandah outside adding to its spaciousness. We felt as though we were in a banqueting hall when we sat down to our meals. Although we were provided with the same food as the other houses, the girls considered it much better, and the small rusty kitchen gas stove came in for many a compliment!

There was a great deal of supposition going on amongst the girls about the alterations being made in Acacia. None of us knew exactly what was happening. Dominating all other considerations was one primary concern. Repeatedly I was asked: 'Are we having doors put on our cubicles?' There was such an eagerness about the question. Up until now they had still only been screened off by a curtain. It was the desire of their lives to have something different. But they became so used to Bolobo, they were really sorry to move back. Part of me was – and part of me wasn't, for although I had not lost my love for the house and it could look cosy and inviting, it was old and grime collected like magic.

We staff were given short notice to clean up Acacia, so we began before the decorators finished, finding ourselves immersed in clouds of dust and a considerable amount of scrubbing.

We had it ready in time and although the girls appreciated all the changes and improvements for the better, the biggest thrill was at getting their wish. Millionaires can have their riches, artists their acclaim, monarchs their kingdoms. Nothing can equal the joy these girls experienced for the gift of one small door which enabled them to shut out the rest of the world!

Chapter 7

WINTERTIME AT EDGWARE

ENTERTAINMENTS

Television arrived at John Grooms in time for the Coronation of Queen Elizabeth II. Not in the houses — that was to develop later but in a small wooden building not far from the factory and behind the concert hall. Big events, like the Coronation, acted like a magnet and the estate was practically deserted. Other than that, television did not prove the overwhelming attraction one would have expected, though it did have its few addicts. Doris was one. Evening after evening would find her rapidly disappearing down the path from Acacia that led to her Elysium. At supper time, whoever was on duty would push the supper drinks in on the trolley and leave the girls to help themselves. It was customary to ask permission if someone wanted their visitor to stay for a cup of tea. Doris was always asking. I did not know she had so many friends! But it was only when demands on milk, sugar, and tea got completely out of hand I discovered why. Trays of tea were disappearing along the path to the television room. You could trace it by the line of spillage. Complaints began coming in from those who had the task of cleaning up the hut next day. But not until I had convinced her I was not supplied with rations for the whole community was the battle won.

Miss Abbot lived outside the estate but acted as relief housemother in emergencies. She also ran a tuck shop in the same hut that housed the television. Here, three times a week in the lunch break, girls could purchase a wide variety of confectionery.

Miss Abbot also repaired the laundry, for Matron never wasted a thing. When linen roller towels which hung in the kitchen, bathroom and cloakroom were past redemption, they

75

were turned into tea towels, worn sheets sides to middles, while hand and bath towels were patched beyond recognition. It was no joke trying to make a fair allocation to the girls, particularly the uncomfortable sides to middle sheets which left a bumpy seam, though I often did penance by giving myself the sorriest of the linen. Perhaps the worst was knowing where to allocate the new sheets, after the old had given their last pathetic whimper, without inviting accusations of favouritism.

This state of affairs had little effect upon the warm regard the girls held towards Matron. Perhaps it was because of the love she showed them in so many ways. She was chief 'Mum' – a tall lady, (in total contrast to diminutive Miss Dean, her predecessor) – wearing a navy blue dress with a white collar and white nurses cap, and a long navy cloak for outdoors, often seen striding round the estate keeping her finger on the pulse of the family heartbeat. Truly, as I had sensed in my first interview with her, she was utterly dedicated in her service to Grooms. She had formerly been a nursing Sister in the Leper Colony of Ruanda until health reasons had brought her home; and if a strong inflexible will, no doubt developed under these circumstances, could sometimes cause difficulties, there was always the underlying sense that she was very caring. Certainly if there were any problems between girls and staff, she could be the diplomatic peacemaker. Girls did not hesitate to go to her with their problems. If there was an outing, she would never retire for the night without seeing everyone was safely back indoors. As the coach drew in, she would be waiting with a wheelchair ready to push the more handicapped girls back to their houses herself.

The girls did not lack for entertainments. They organised outings among themselves. Coach trips worked out to only a few shillings per head. Lorraine remembers her first outing, which was also her first view of the sea. It was to Southend. All day long she never got tired of parading up and down looking at the sea sparkling in the clear sunshine. There were concerts and film shows held in the concert hall, though some of the films were rather antiquated. Even for the fifties, early films of Will Hay, with poor acoustics, were rather out of date.

There were pianos in some of the houses. There had been one in Lilac and Ivy Lewis, who sang and played beautifully, would gather the girls around her for a sing-song. This was a particular relaxation for Friday evenings and nothing could be more 'homely' than that.

But best of all was John Grooms' own choir and dramatic society, led by a team of dedicated women who would travel from their work of an evening, giving freely of their time and perform absolute wonders drawing out talents the girls never knew they possessed. Miss Miller gave years of service playing the piano. Olive Goodson conducted, while Hilda Partridge produced the shows, her two friends creating the top rate costumes.

I have heard it said that these shows were worthy of professional status, and I can vouch for it, for each had the stamp of professionalism upon it. The concert hall was always packed to capacity in the two shows performed, one on a weeknight, and the other on Saturdays. Looking back now it seems a pity that, apart from a retiring collection towards the cost of the costumes, entrance was free. Even a small charge would have brought in a substantial figure, but giving enjoyment was the only reward asked. It was open to any who cared to join. There were no restrictions. The girls who belonged never had a dull moment. Rehearsals sometimes took place more than once a week, plus another evening for choir practice and as a concert drew near it would involve every evening.

Centenary concert – Edgware

'Cries of Old London'

Amongst a variety of performances was a Dutch show; a gypsy one with a real gypsy caravan on stage; cries of old London, a colourful production which symbolised early John Grooms with its basket of flowers and girls dressed in blouses, long skirts, aprons, shawls and straw hats representing flower sellers of long ago. One year there was a pantomime, 'Babes in the Wood', a superb production. Different girls stand out with their particular talent: Nellie with her comic songs ('I'm a lonely little petunia in an onion patch' being one of them); Ivy, Rose, Annie, and Violet, with their solos; Alex's monologues; Daisy with her yodelling; Lorraine with her diversity of accents in the mini-plays. These had their 'near misses' like the sketch where Lorraine was meant to be strap-hanging on the tube. The train lurched and she was meant to be found sitting on the lap of the person behind her. But there was no lap there! To have sat on an empty chair would have caused calamity because it was too low for her. The incident was saved by the split second timing of the girl in the next chair sliding speedily into the vacant place.

In the 'Toy Symphony', she played the 'nightingale'. The warble was made by filling the whistle with water but the water kept running out and she was left making frantic efforts to get the whistle refilled before her next turn to join in. In spite of the raincoat wrapped round her she was drenched!

John Grooms choir at Edgware

There was plenty of fun, but there were sad moments. The beauty of the entertainment lay in its outgoingness, giving service to others transcending disability. They would often give concerts at hospitals, old peoples homes and in church halls. A concert at an old people's home stands out in my memory. There was a very sick young man living amongst them for lack of suitable accommodation elsewhere. The girls rendered a version of 'Just a Song at Twilight'. After they had sung it, this young man was able to make signs he wanted them to repeat it. If the singing was inspired before, it was doubly so now. There was a strange hush when it ended. We heard that he died a few days later.

They loved going to the 'Star and Garter', the disabled ex-servicemen's home at Richmond. At tea afterwards, some helped to feed those who could not feed themselves.

CHRISTMAS

After the summer holidays, rehearsals would start for the Christmas concert. This would be given about the end of November and herald the start of our Christmas preparations. Actually, in Acacia, the countdown was given by Doris. Immediately she came back from her summer break in Yorkshire,

I would be informed of the exact number of weeks and days to when she would be returning. When the M1 came under construction she took such an interest in it we began to wonder if she had shares in it!

'Soon be eating fish and chips on the road,' she once announced cheerfully.

'On the road, Doris?' Miss Delves exclaimed in feigned horror. 'No newspaper?'

A large percentage of the flowers were going to well-known stores like Selfridges and John Lewis and to film studios; also Butlins at Bognor when it first opened used Grooms flowers as background decoration to their swimming pool. The annual Christmas exhibition of flowers began in the factory in late November and went on until just before Christmas. Many coach parties came to view and buy the flowers. The milling crowds and excited chatter gave it a full festive flavour, even more so when, because of its popularity, the exhibition had to be transferred to our large concert hall. I thought I was suffering illusions one rather misty dank day when, approaching the hall and from the light streaming out, I saw multi-coloured roses 'blooming' on the bushes outside! Someone had expertly tied on the artificial ones giving us, like memories, 'roses in December.'

Some of these coach parties had visited earlier in the year, as organised parties of 40 or more people from churches or clubs; visiting the factory and houses was another regular weekly feature. Individual friendships which have lasted a lifetime have been formed between some members of these parties and the girls.

In the houses we took it in turns to do the catering. Sandwiches and cakes were prepared in the main kitchen, but house staff made the tea, set the tables and found the extra chairs. We knew the visitors were approaching by the sound of voices and laughter. In they would troop, trying to find somewhere to put the flowers they had bought, for it was a squash trying to accommodate them all. Finally they would be seated and grateful for a cup of tea.

When tea was almost over, Mr. Walter Groom, in charge of these parties and nephew of the founder, would begin telling them all about the work and his Uncle John. He seemed to have a kind of charisma that held their complete attention, his whole manner genial to the staff as well as to the parties. I have never seen him otherwise and he would never fail to thank the staff for their help. It could be a scurry afterwards, getting the room back in order, tables laid and a meal ready for the girls when they came in, but we always managed it.

The Salvation Army Band began paying us a visit at Christmas. The first year they played in the grounds, but it wasn't near enough for some of the girls, so in future they came into each house and played a carol or two. In Acacia they usually positioned themselves in the short corridor outside my room. One evening I was wrapping up Christmas presents unaware the band was on its way, but I soon knew it had arrived when the loud blast of a trumpet outside my door nearly deafened me proclaiming 'Silent Night'!

There were abundant invitations to parties held at local churches, or to nativity plays. The most popular nativity play was the one given by the Polytechnic in Regent Street, London involving a coach outing to get there. Towards my latter years, there would be a festival of carols by candlelight given in the Nursing Home by Sister Hall and Miss Wheatley. It would be absolutely crowded, for those two worked well as a team and were instrumental in reaching the hearts of many a resident with the gospel where the rest of us couldn't.

At the beginning of December we turned into a GPO of our own as cards and parcels began pouring in. It was an unwritten law that I never touched the girls' post, either now or at any other time in the year. They enjoyed collecting their own and found pleasure in staggering back under a weight of parcels it would have been much easier for an able-bodied person to carry.

The majority of the residents went away for Christmas, so those remaining moved into the two houses on the estate still open. Staff and houses took it in turns for Christmas duty while the girls settled among themselves who would occupy their cubicle while they were away, always an amicable arrangement.

Most who had relatives and friends would visit them at this time of year, but those who were left generally had nowhere to go and, for me, that brought Christmas into its true perspective when it was my turn to look after them. I cannot describe the wonderful spirit and atmosphere that pervaded those few days that made any other reward unnecessary and the hard work negligible.

Whether Acacia was open or not, I always liked to make an early beginning with the decorations so that those going away might have a chance to enjoy them. When one year one of my non-church going girls said to me, 'you can't help seeing the true meaning of Christmas through our decorations,' I knew I had achieved exactly what I had aimed for, not mere tinselling.

After breakfast on Christmas morning, those who could went to church and a bit later Matron would come and wish us all a happy Christmas. Then the giving and unwrapping of presents would begin. It was a delight to see the joy a smallest gift could bring. Miss Delves' head and mine were on a swivel trying to look at the gifts thrust under our noses to investigate. Gradually, we began to get lost under a mound of wrapping paper we thought we would never be able to clear away, but somehow we did.

Christmas dinner was a lavish one which Miss Delves and I prepared between us. We sat round the fire afterwards listening to the Wilfred Pickles programme on the radio. Jellies, fruit, iced cake and many other dainties followed for tea. Best of all was sitting round the fire in the evening, with the room darkened and curtains drawn back for the multi-coloured lights of the Christmas tree to shine out. We would sing carols or reminisce about old times. It was particularly interesting hearing of the Sekforde Street time from the older girls.

This would be the pattern for the rest of the Christmas period, before the others began coming back, leaving a glowing memory to look back upon.

Many kindnesses were received throughout the year from people living adjacent to the estate, who were formed into the Edgware 'Friends of John Grooms' in 1970 by Lady Joan Laing. Since then these Friends have worked tirelessly to raise money for buildings and equipment to enhance the lives of the residents. Many of those involved initially are still active and on the sad death of Lady Laing in 1981 her place as Chairman was taken by Mrs. Marina Hobson. As with all fund-raising, many ingenious schemes have been devised including golf tournaments, plant sales and lunches and dinners with a variety of themes.

Over the years, various motor vehicles have been purchased to enable the disabled residents to go to places of their choice, and it is true to say that requests for special items of equipment have never gone unanswered. What is equally important – if not more so – has been the **personal** involvement of the Edgware Friends of John Grooms with those living on the estate. Every resident receives a Christmas present and a birthday card each year and there have been many lunches and parties at Mr. and Mrs. Hobson's lovely home.

Mrs. Joan Pacheco has been secretary to the Edgware Friends of John Grooms since its inception until 1990 when she stepped

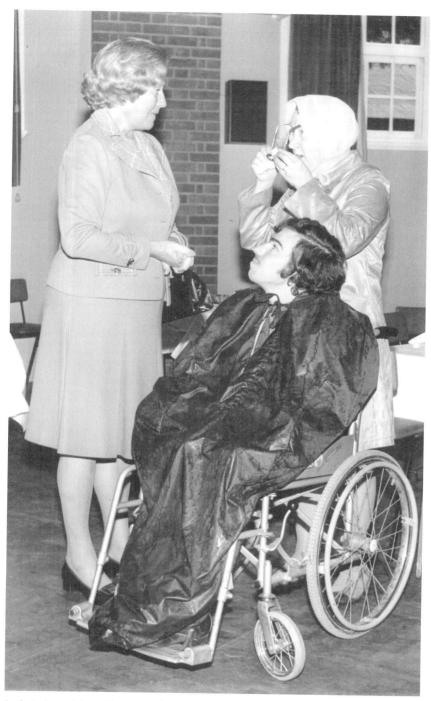

Lady Laing with residents at Edgware

Esther Rantzen presents new bus from Edgware Friends of John Grooms

into Mrs. Hobson's shoes as Chairman. Mrs. Yvonne Fairweather, Vice-Chairman of the Association, has always been very actively involved with the residents at Edgware and says that she is proud to count them amongst her personal friends. It is quite amazing to note that in the past twenty-five years, The Edgware Friends have raised in excess of £250,000 – a truly wonderful record!

MOBILITY

January often heralded a season of snow. Picturesque it might have been, but something to dread in a very real way when you are disabled. For the majority it could mean confinement to the estate for weeks.

The girls had to get backwards and forwards to the factory somehow each day. No mean achievement, for however much the paths were cleared, it always managed to snow just as they were due in – or it seemed that way. A heavy snowfall overnight would have staff pitching in to make a clearance, but it was exhausting work and there wasn't time to deal with the icy patches left. Spraying salt was an effective, if expensive, way of dealing with the problem, but it took too much and we soon ran out. So we house staff would down tools once more and combine our efforts to get the residents to and from work. Matron in her usual caring way was always first on the scene.

Pushing wheelchairs backwards and forwards in the snow would have been simplified could they have had runners fitted in place of wheels – one slight deviation from the path and wheels refused to go round, sunk in a depth of snow.

If we ran out of wheelchairs, we could offer an arm to someone more hardy stumbling along unsupported. Glenys liked an arm to cling to, but since she was on the plump side and I wasn't, we resembled a drunken procession staggering along, especially when I became embedded in the soft snow surrounding the path where her leaning had impelled me!

Burst pipes are the bane of any household. They were the bane of our houses on the estate. One bitterly cold winter, even with the radiators full on, the kitchen in Acacia stayed as ice cold as a refrigerator. Water froze in the tap and had to be supplied from neighbouring buildings which had fared better than us. The large pipe running the length of the outside wall overlooking the main road had at some unseen time overflowed, turning into a sheet of ice as it cascaded down. Passers-by gazed spellbound at this exquisite ice waterfall. As soon as the thaw set in, a fountain of water spouts began as one pipe after another burst. The shout of 'burst pipe' was as the sound of 'donkeys' to Betsy Trotwood – a call to action.

The assistant's room was a bit on the dark side. It now assumed an expression of continuous weeping, where the burst pipes from the bathroom overhead had sent trickles through the ceiling and down the walls, leaving a permanent stain of tears!

Snow or no snow, our annual New Year party in the house was never missed. Each house gave a party and the girls were allowed to invite one friend each. We would sit down to a meal, an ample one, in Acacia more like another Christmas dinner; but it was the fun and fellowship that made these evenings so worthwhile.

Someone enterprising enough would plan and lead the games. Not a minute of the evening was wasted. There were simple parlour games and team games; musical parcel, musical chairs, musical hats, 'fanning the fish' (a team game where a paper fish had to be flapped along the floor to the front of the queue); or try eating a piece of chocolate with a fork! There would be dressing up for charades, sketches done by the girls themselves and, of course, the inevitable sing-song. These were simple pleasures a more sophisticated society may have pushed out of sight, but for us they fitted into our home life, bringing another bright glow to the winter season. Soon it would be spring before we realised it and so on into summer.

Princess Alexandra came on a visit once. Everything was

A royal visit to Edgware in the 1950's by HRH Princess Alexandra – with Geoffrey Parker (Principal), and two of the disabled young women

made spick and span. In the factory, the girls unable to do the more interesting work were kept to the back. The best work and workers were well to the fore. But ignoring the 'official' approach, our friendly Princess squeezed her way through all the narrow spaces and spoke to **everyone**. No girl was left out. She showed a real interest in what each one was doing, and really loved the spray of artificial flowers presented to her.

In the nineteen fifties, mobility for disabled people at John

Doris and Hetty plan their route with their 'Tippens'

Grooms who could not use public transport was restricted to the rare few who possessed self-propelling three-wheeler chairs. Ethel Lee was one. Regularly each Sunday morning, wet or shine, would see her propelling her way along the Watford by-pass to the Methodist Church at Mill Hill. Ethel was no longer young and it was a long haul, but she rarely missed.

Hetty was another who had a three-wheeler, only hers was motorised. Stiff jointed, and unable to recline comfortably because of the steel jacket she wore, she performed incredible feats of driving herself everywhere in that motorised chair. Then, still amazingly bright after a tiring journey, she would come in cheerily to tell of her exploits. Even a tarpaulin cover could not entirely protect her from the pouring rain, yet she could still return with a broad smile however drenched. Her three-wheeler was her freedom and meant everything to her.

For a few pounds Lorraine had purchased one of these three-wheelers from one of the other girls no longer requiring it. I tried to persuade her to apply for a ministry motor chair as these were just coming into fashion. She had doubts. First she thought she would not qualify and then she feared she would lack courage to take it on the road. Finally, thinking no harm could come by merely enquiring, she applied to the NHS. In no time at all, to her complete astonishment, and the astonishment of the other girls, she became the owner of a shiny ice blue three-wheeler vehicle. She had only been expecting an open trike like Hetty's.

A Tippen, it was called. I remember the morning it was delivered excitedly sending her down a note ready for when she came in from the factory, for Matron had allowed it to be garaged in a disused shed near Acacia and close by the handyman's workshop. Duly she arrived to inspect it, a contingent of girls following. They spent a long time delighting in this 'thing of beauty' as it was to them, little realising perhaps that this was the dawn of a new era of motorised freedom for them all. So many were to acquire them later that special garages were eventually to be built by the Stoneyfields Lane entrance.

Log book and instructions arrived the following day and a few days later an official representative arrived to show her how to drive it. Lorraine sat in the driving seat and he sat crouched beside her explaining the controls while she wobbled the vehicle round the grounds. She thanked him for showing her, asked when the next lesson would be and was stunned when he told her there wouldn't be any more. That was it!

'Study your driving manual,' he said, 'and you'll be all right.' Fortunately for Lorraine, an able-bodied friend came to the rescue and gave her several lessons.

Hetty also had a similar motor tricycle now and, being a more experienced driver, would often escort Lorraine on journeys familiar to her but not to Lorraine. Their adventures were legion. A shopping expedition into Mill Hill ended up disastrously. They enjoyed the excursion but, coming back and turning into the entrance of the estate, everything began wavering before Lorraine's eyes. In a split second of shock, she realised the trike was turning over and an instinctive reaction to fear of fire made her instantly turn off the ignition.

The next thing she knew, faces were looking down at her through a hole in the perspex window where her arm had gone through. She was totally unhurt; nonetheless she had now discovered why they were referred to as 'Flippin' Tippens'! The front wheel had skidded on a patch of oil left on the surface from a recent retarring of the road. Once that happened, turning over was inevitable.

Anxious bystanders lifted the vehicle back to position with Lorraine sitting in it. One bystander tried to make her drive straight on. If she didn't, he said, she wouldn't find the courage later and Sister Hall arriving on the scene gave her backing to this

Helen at work – painting handmade flower petals

wise advice, so she was encouraged to do it.

Soon she was driving happily around again. One Friday evening when she and Hetty were both going to spend the weekend with their respective relations, they started off badly. It took twenty minutes getting off the estate into the rush hour traffic on the Edgware Way. They reached Hanger Lane on the North Circular, when they were caught in another traffic jam. This caused Hetty's engine to stall. A car load of Americans was following and, seeing Hetty was having difficulty, one obligingly jumped out to give her vehicle a push-start. Four times the engine stalled and each time a different American came to the rescue.

Eventually they were out of the traffic congestion, but now it was Lorraine's turn to break down. The Americans, unfortunately, had gone on ahead. So had Hetty – but only to get help. How relieved Lorraine was to see her slowly returning with a policeman following, who soon located the trouble and had her started again.

On another occasion, in the process of breaking down, she had crawled round Marble Arch at five miles per hour escorting a fleet of buses steered by their patient drivers, had come to a halt in the middle of busy roads and then been hauled into a breakdown van to sit in a tangle of wireless wires, while her temperamental vehicle, like a small blue fly dangling on the end of a fishing line, had been towed forlornly away. Yet she never lost her joy in driving and her legion of prayers for help were always answered.

Helen was another who benefitted from having a motor chair, a specially adapted one for she had no hands. She was of small build, having similar disabilities to a thalidomide victim. But she was also extremely talented, making all her own clothes beautifully styled, exquisitely stitched; and there was nothing amateurish about the paintings she did by mouth. Once she travelled by plane, all on her own, to visit friends in Germany. She wrote a diary on her travels and held us completely enthralled when she read it out to us at one of our Thursday evening meetings.

And the freedom of the Motability scheme opened up travel opportunities for many more as time went by, for girls who had never dreamed they had a capability for driving.

RHUBARB AND ROSEWAY!

I had now been in Acacia seven years and was without any inkling that things were going to change. I had spent a short time in hospital and had gone back to my home in London to recuperate when, one morning, I received a letter from Matron that put me in a turmoil of indecision. Would I consider becoming housemother of Roseway – the house that had charmed me during our temporary respite from Acacia, now renovated and housing the older women still working but not so many years from retirement.

I was only given a very short time to make up my mind. Acacia had become my home. I did not want to leave it, but at the same time recognised the seniority of the situation and the compliment of being asked. Although I considered it prayerfully, I had no clear sense of the right thing to do. But it did come into my mind the kind of tranquillity I had encountered on my visits there. These older girls all had their own rooms, and I imagined being a housemother there would be quieter and less demanding, a consideration I doubt would have entered my head had I been in full health.

The time was not ready for me to take over when I returned from sick leave, which was just as well since I was not yet fully fit. So I was glad to do part time in the Nursing Home. It was sadness all round going into Acacia – worse for the girls because, although

I was unaware of it at the time, Miss Delves would soon be leaving them too. She was moving to Orchard House to be on the staff there. So, in a way, Acacia was losing two 'mums' almost simultaneously.

The Nursing Home was run by a uniformed Sister and a white coated assistant. An orderly and a daily help comprised the rest of the staff. It had two wards holding five beds each, with a two bedded isolation ward a step down from the kitchen quarters.

Scripture reading and prayers for those well enough to join in were the order of the day. On one occasion each girl was being asked to state her favourite portion of Scripture. Rose happened to be out of the ward at the time the discussion first began. When she returned, she was faced with a question without the nature of the subject being explained.

'What's your favourite portion, Rose?'

'Rhubarb and custard,' replied Rose, promptly and innocently. It was plain to see the channel her thoughts were on – not on spiritual food!

It was coming up for a Bank Holiday during my stay. Sister Hall and Miss Wheatley were both very grateful when I offered to be on duty so they could both be away for a night. There was only one patient to look after and Matron was on call for emergencies.

I slept above the boiler room and was used to the boiler throbbing. It soothed like a lullaby until it switched itself off and restarted automatically in the morning, a huge old monster. This particular evening, having nothing more to do once Lily – the patient – had settled down, I retired early. I slept fitfully, disturbed by a premonition something was going to happen, and awoke at dawn with a curious sense of expectancy. The boiler began throbbing as it switched itself on, lulling me off to sleep again, until I awoke uneasily, sure the throbbing was getting louder. There was a report like a canon and a foul smell began seeping up towards me. I shot down the stairs. Thick acrid smoke was pouring out from the kitchen. Choking, I forced my way through the black fog to get to the boiler below – which was still burbling away angrily – to switch it off. But the kitchen door leading down to it was tightly jammed from the first explosion.

Because I was suffocating, and could stand no more, I raced back to the corridor for air. Only in the nick of time. There was an explosion that rocked the building, followed by the sound of splintering wood and glass. The stout, strongly made door I had just been struggling to open lay in shattered fragments all over the

The lounge at Lilac

floor. I phoned desperately for help and ran to my lone patient in the ward furthest away. She was rocking backwards and forwards in fright.

'We still have a purpose in life because we're still here!' I comforted weakly. Oddly enough, it did seem to calm her down. Through the window I saw the caretaker approaching. He forced his way through the wreckage and braved the boiler. Only when its angry hum was silenced did I breathe a sigh of relief.

Then began a survey of the damage and cleaning up began. The isolation door and windows had been blasted open, so had the back door, but not a pane of glass was touched, neither was a cup, saucer or plate broken. Such was the freak of the blast, it had left only one smashed door. But everywhere was smothered in thick soot; the kitchen shelves I had laboriously scrubbed during the week, the gas stove and table, and the red tiled floor had completely changed colour. It took days to clear; it was in the air, a pall of soot resettling as soon as the top layer was removed.

Doubtless a reason for the explosion was discovered. At the time it was only a mystery. It was almost a relief to start in Roseway after that.

But if a quiet house, with girls disappearing into the peace of their own rooms immediately a meal was over made for tranquillity, then I did not find it very satisfying and all that had charmed me in the old house had been completely lost in its renovations.

The lounge was separate from the dining room and rarely used, except by the two or three stalwarts who watched the television recently installed. In Acacia the younger ones had always been around, and I missed them. There had been so much scope for helping them, like the new girl who had come three weeks after I had started life in Acacia. On the morning she arrived I had been laying up the tables for lunch while she sat and watched me, silently shedding tears. She was sixteen, severely afflicted, and it was all the more poignant she could not fully communicate her distress because of an inability of the facial muscles to express what she was truly feeling.

I sought inwardly to be able to say something that would be of any comfort and, with a flash of insight, told her I understood. A newcomer in the house myself, I too was homesick (as indeed I was – for Lilac). Identifying seemed to cheer her up, and the girls did all they could to make her feel at home and gain the confidence she needed for going out and about.

Nevertheless, she did not seem able to overcome boredom and restlessness. The disability in her hands rendered her unable to take part in the more skilled flower making, but the 'pin' work she was given to do was inadequate for her active brain.

I felt she needed some kind of stimulus, so I suggested she got down to some writing and she was keen to do this. I didn't just have literary development in mind. I tried to choose subject

Roseway verandah

matter that would make her think more deeply about her faith – for she had been converted through a Billy Graham relay at the Parish church. She would trot off quite happily to the Quiet Room and come back with the finished project. The first one was along the line of 'My last day on earth'. How I expected a sixteen-year-old to cope with material of this kind, I don't know, and it is a standing joke between us to this day!

The next step was to get her reading. From a tardy start, she began to enjoy some of the well known classics. She liked to write poems and a couple of these were published in a magazine for disabled people. Eventually, she was to leave John Grooms and, after a stormy beginning, make her own way in the world. Later a course in the Open University opened the way for her to do some teaching.

This kind of service obviously wasn't going to be needed in Roseway. Nonetheless, it was brought home to me how God plans ahead of us. I could not regret leaving Acacia for long because Acacia – the home I had known – would have left me! A lift was installed and those less disabled were moved out to make room for the more severely handicapped ones who had difficulty climbing stairs. Some Acacia girls eventually left Grooms altogether.

Dorothy working on the Christmas lights contract

So I settled in Roseway. I appreciated my private living quarters because I had my own front door and an open fireplace in the small sitting room, which meant I could have the cosiness of a coal fire if I wanted it. I gave a small party inviting a few friends and, after a thoroughly happy social evening, the unlived-in lounge seemed to take on a different aspect. It taught me what a 'house warming' is all about.

Olive would bring her typewriter down to the empty dining room of an evening and laboriously tap out her letters with hands weakened by polio, alternating it with a dive into the lounge from time to time to view what was on television. A thorough chatterbox, the minute she saw me she would break from her typing to launch into an interesting discussion, usually bringing in our faith. Then Hetty, who I had known from Lilac days, moved in. On Saturdays she would sit and chat while she made up her sandwiches for the Disabled Drivers Association meetings.

The years seemed to slip by and by the mid 1960's the old ways were being disturbed by the winds of change. Lilac and Laburnum closed down to become Dainesmead, altered to accommodate more severely disabled young women in wheelchairs of the motorised kind. Although some of them would like to have done so, they did not work in the factory at that time. The 'girls' of Lilac and Laburnum had to move to other houses, and it was very unsettling for them.

Imported artificial flowers and the advent of plastic were reducing the demand for Grooms material ones, so supplementary contract work was being taken on in the factory. Helping the British Legion with the Armistice poppies, testing and packing Christmas tree lights, making and packing Christmas crackers, folding and boxing 'pop-up' birthday cards, soldering work and pressed rivets for a telephone company – these were a sample of the new work being taken on.

As for me, a new channel of service was opening up. I needed more time for my writing. So – not without a lot of heartache – I left Grooms.

Or I thought I had! Later years were to bring some surprises!

Chapter 8

HOMES FOR THE CHILDREN

Running ever parallel with his concern for the disabled flower-seller, John Groom was also consumed with compassion for deprived and orphaned children. He lived in an age when mothers were dying in childbirth from diseases caused by absence of sanitation and severe poverty. Every day he met uncared-for orphans on the streets of London and, although he drew them into the warmth and care of the Mission and Sunday School, he knew it was not enough. The light dawned on what he must do one day in 1888 when, feeling such pity for three little Londoners he found roaming the streets, he took them into his own home. To effect any real solution to this problem he must open for them, and for those like them, an entirely new way of life in a home right away from the dingy streets that was their home now. The time had come to act.

This idea was prospered by the advent of the railways. By 1900 the main line network was almost complete and, with Liverpool Street Station not too far from Clerkenwell, a speedy and cheap means of transport to a health-giving part of the Essex coast was made available. A new and suitable property was offered to the Grooms Council at a reasonable price at Clacton-on-Sea. It was a small house, standing in its own grounds, which could well be enlarged by building on dormitories, dining and play rooms, where thirty to forty children could be accommodated and there would still be room for further extensions should they prove necessary.

But John stood by his deep inner conviction to undertake no new commitment without first having the money to pay for it, and funds were exhausted. Nonetheless, he and his helpers held strongly to the faith that the money would come if God intended them to purchase the house.

And it did come!

An anonymous gift of £1,000 enabled them to purchase not only the property, but an adjacent piece of land on which they were later to build five more homes. All they knew of the donor was that she was a single lady named 'Violet', and she had the honour of having one of these homes named after her.

The building and its extension was opened on April 19th 1890, and was soon taking in deserted children, orphans, those rescued out of the hands of ruthless parents using them for their own ends and, even more poignantly, those heartbreakingly handed over by mothers giving way under the strain of daily living and who were longing for a better future for their children. Young mothers, who had been deserted by the fathers of their children, were also offered refuge and trained for either domestic service or a business career.

Three years after the first house had been opened there were 100 girls in the Homes. Each home was named after a flower – Violet, Snowdrop, Forget-me-not, Buttercup, Daisy, Bluebell and Lobelia, and still there was a need for more homes. Generous gifts from friends enabled the Council to purchase a larger piece of land on the other side of the road, and plans were drawn up for six more houses to be built. But without any more money available to continue the work, they could only pray and wait in faith for something to happen. And one morning it did!

In the post came an envelope containing two five hundred pound bank notes, addressed to 'The Founder' and with the brief message 'Towards the new houses at Clacton-on-Sea.' There was no name or address or any other trace of the sender. But the story does not end there. Grooms expressed their thanks in two religious journals, and some time afterwards came another envelope from the same donor. Inside was a question. 'How much money is required to build and furnish the five houses needed? Send particulars to bankers.'

The reply was sent: '£5,000 is needed.' A mere two days later a banker's draft was received for the whole amount, a receipt sent through the banker to the client with a letter of thanks, and the work was immediately put in hand; Wallflower, Lily, Mignonette, Rosebud and Pansy were eventually built and occupied. Still there was more to come!

'Violet' came to the fore again with a large sum of money which, when invested, provided sufficient interest to pay rates, decoration and repairs as required on all these new homes. Thus

A cartload of youngsters – outside Rosebud

a small settlement was established which was soon known as The Flower Village.

Each home accommodated twenty girls with a Matron or Housemother in charge, with two home helps. These helps were often older girls, for all who were able-bodied were trained for a future career in domestic service. There was little option in those early days and it offered a vast improvement to what life would have been without that option. They could look forward to a comfortable home with the confidence of being self-supporting. They had a full year of training after leaving school and were then found suitable employment. Demand for their services became greater than the number of girls available to accept positions. Those disabled and physically unfit for domestic service were sent to the workrooms at Clerkenwell (later to Edgware).

The houses were run as family homes, girls being of varying ages, those from eleven years old taking responsibility for the care of the little ones. One elderly lady says: 'I went to Clacton as a baby with my twin sister. I owe everything to the work of John Groom, and thank God I was sent there.'

Another quotes a punishment meted out to her: 'I have good reason for remembering when we changed from gas lighting to electric lighting. The novelty of having a light at the touch of a switch was too tempting to ignore. What fun we had, only to discover that our housemother was across the road watching us. We had thought she was safely at the church taking her Band of Hope class. Our punishment was to put our Saturday penny in the collecting box for a month to help pay for the electricity we had used. As my father and mother had both died by the time I was five years old I often wonder how different life would have been for my younger sister and me if it had not been for John Groom. We both have appreciated that we were able to go and live at Clacton with its healthy sea air.'

Another elderly lady gives insight on her childhood at Clacton: 'We wore calico nighties and getting into bed between icy cold calico sheets was like getting into a cold water bath. However some bright spark solved the problem by sneaking into the kitchen when no one was about and smuggling the oven shelf up to the dormitory wrapped in a cloth. She would warm her own bed, then pass it on to the next bed, and then to the next, until there was very little warmth left in it by the time it got to the last person. We progressed from oven shelf to bricks which had been left about by workmen. We would get them and put them in the kitchen oven to get hot, then would watch for an opportunity to sneak to the kitchen and get our lovely hot foot warmers, until one girl overslept, had her bedclothes stripped off and the brick fell on the floor and put paid to that!'

They were obviously a lively crowd, getting the maximum amount of enjoyment from life. They would march up and down the dormitory singing 'MacNamara's Band' to the accompaniment of the blowing of whistles, blowing through the teeth of a comb covered with tissue paper, and banging on a biscuit tin with a couple of sticks, until Matron clapped her hands sharply and told them to get off to sleep and the noise ceased abruptly.

A few years later, in the early twenties, a very clear picture of what life was like at the Clacton Homes is portrayed by Mrs. Marjorie Ward, now living at Bluntisham in Huntingdonshire who, together with her twin sister, was taken to live there after their mother died, though sadly, only a year later her sister died too.

Marjorie's earliest memory stems from the age of three or four when she recalls sitting on the knee of the black clad, hobble skirted housemother –always known as 'Mother' to the children – being jiggled up and down while watching the snowflakes coming down outside and worrying whether she was going to receive a smacking at bath time. For some reason or other this seems to have been a punishment inflicted upon her a lot, until a new 'Mother' took over and she settled in much more happily.

'Rosebud' was her home for a time and the other homes were no doubt similar in their furnishings. Downstairs was the mother's sitting room. At the back of that was the kitchen, with its big Welsh dresser and black pot-board underneath for the kettles, steamers and saucepans. The hallway was narrower at the rear because of the broom cupboard, which was partly under the stairs, but the front of the hall was wider with a large ornate front door.

On the other side of the hall was the dining-cum-play room, and leading off from here was the scullery and downstairs toilet. The back yard was a quadrangle with four sets of three steps leading into toilet, scullery, kitchen and coalhouse. A centre drain in the yard took care of the rainwater, although many times it flooded during heavy rainstorms.

The scullery contained a sink, big wooden draining boards and a large shoe rack, which held all the children's shoes. There were twenty four pairs and two twelve-year-old girls were allotted turns to clean all the shoes every night directly after tea. They were never allowed in the dining-cum-play room in their outdoor shoes. At nine years of age each child was given a job to do morning and evening. At eleven they were each responsible for one of the little ones, inspecting their clothing for missing buttons, or for holes in their socks. If there were, the minder would then have to repair the item for the next day.

Marjorie narrates as follows:

'We were awakened at 6.30am each morning, We stripped and made our beds. Breakfast was at 7.30am. After that I had to clean all the brasses in the house. I didn't mind this too much as you could get on with the job without waiting for your partner to catch up with you as happened in dusting and sweeping dormitories. The white quilts on the beds had to be tucked in hospital fashion and all the bottoms of the beds had to be in a straight line. Another job I had to do was to clean the downstairs toilet. This was done with earth and nothing else. All the flights of steps in the yard had to be scrubbed, and on Saturdays the yard had to be swilled down with soda water and scrubbed with a hard broom.

Each Sunday we had to attend one of four local churches; Baptist, Wesleyan, Zion Church and Christ Church. I favoured the Baptist Church. When Uncle Ted (Mr. Cooke) came down to Clacton during the summer, he always attended there. Once he came and sat beside me. How thrilled I was, and how we all loved that warm-hearted man! Each Monday when he was due to come, we would watch out for him with bated breath, then vie with each other in asking if we could clean and polish his Austin Morris.

We would all gather round him at night while he chatted to us and told us a story in answer to our clamour for one. This lovely man must have been so tired with all the travelling he did, but he never failed in telling us at least one tale. During the winter months, when his visits were less frequent, we would sometimes be privileged to sit at his feet before a glowing fire in Mother's sitting room where once again we would demand a story. He would make up one about an oddity called "Pappymondus", who turned out to be a stupid fellow doing all the wrong things, so that we all ended up laughing our heads off!

Sunday we had our own evening service, and one particular Sunday when Uncle Ted was going to speak, Mother told me I would be stopped from going to hear him because I had misbehaved but, after pleading with her, she gave in and I went. But Oh dear me! Uncle Ted's subject was about faces. People's faces, and how he could read them and tell what sort of face it was, whether the owner was happy, miserable, or whether they had been naughty. Later, when he stood at the door saying goodnight to each of us, I put my hands over my face and rushed past him!'

Christmas was a very exciting time, with preparations going on weeks ahead, and everyone joining in the decorating. Marjorie's bed was under the window and she loved to lie and listen to the Salvation Army Band playing carols in the road outside. On Christmas Eve, stockings were hung up for Father Christmas to fill and each child received a sugar mouse, some form of confectionery and a game. Older girls received a diary, perfume, an autograph book, or some other small useful gift.

On Christmas morning, the house girls gave the children breakfast in bed. This was a way to keep them upstairs so that the tables could be prepared for the Christmas dinner. After they had had breakfast they would get into bed with each other and read stories or play games until Mother told them they could get dressed. They would put on their Sunday best and then excitedly watch out of the big front windows awaiting their turn for Father and Mother Christmas to stop outside their house with their big cart. This cart bore the parcels that relatives sent to their children at Grooms. Father and Mother Christmas were two of the workers dressed up and they used to come along the crescent ringing their bell. The parcels were taken into the warm kitchen, put on the big white scrubbed table, and then Mother would hand them out. Poor Marjorie had no one to send her anything until Mother persuaded a friend to send her a parcel, and what a thrill it was for her that Christmas!

They all sat down to dinner and the huge turkey was carved by Uncle Alfred (John Groom's son). Marjorie continues:

'We would sing a carol to him before jollifications started. After dinner, we were sent up to rest on our beds while the washing up was done, then we went on to a big party held in the Holiday Home across the road. This Holiday Home was built especially for use of the girls and women working in the Crippleage to have an annual break by the seaside. The tables were all laid out, two houses to a table, and a sumptuous tea was followed by all the old familiar games, Postman's Knock, Blindman's Buff, Oranges and Lemons, Musical Chairs and so forth. At eight o'clock, Father Christmas appeared again to hand out presents.

Boxing Day we did not get up until nine or ten and it was Christmas all over again. We went back to the Holiday Home in the afternoon and were entertained by a concert group. At the end of their performance we were each given a whole sixpence (2 ½p)! And Christmas was not over yet! Each house planned its own party and we were allowed one friend each as a guest. As I look back after all these years, I cannot but marvel again and again at the tremendous amount of work that went into giving us such wonderful Christmases.'

From the first Tuesday in June to the first Tuesday in September, there were weekly fete days to raise funds for the orphanage. The girls practised hard all the year round. Marjorie cherishes to this day a memory of the time they danced all the dances of the Commonwealth and finalised the display by singing 'Land of Hope and Glory'. It proved so popular they were asked to repeat the programme, which they did, and immediately the finale was reached, a man jumped on to the platform and began conducting the music. He had his pianist with him. They were the famous conductor and his equally famous brother, Eric and Stanford Robinson. Everyone joined in the chorus, for these fete days were extremely popular and encouraged vast crowds. There were tiers of seats, rather like a football stadium from where events could be watched.

Alfred Groom and a Mr. Abbott used to be in charge of the games. There were the chariot races. These were boxes on wheels with their handles decorated with artificial flowers. Wives and girlfriends would sit in the boxes and their men folk would race them. There were relay races, tug-of-war (six men against twelve girls, and Mr. Groom and Mr. Abbot would choose the team, making sure they chose the less-hefty looking men!) Needless to say the girls always won!

PT display at Fete Day, Clacton, 1905

The highlight of the evening, at 10pm, was in taking part in the Fire Display. The older girls would put night-dresses over their day clothes and stand in the corridor of the Holiday Home while Mr. Nash, foreman of the workers on the estate, lit the fireworks which had been erected on the outside walls and balcony. The first bang would send the girls rushing onto the balcony to yell 'Fire!' This would incite the workers, dressed up as firemen, to come running with a ladder. They would rush onto the balcony to let down the chute, which was in the middle of the balcony. The girls would be pushed down the chute head first, to be rescued by another fireman at the bottom, and then rush back into the building yelling 'Fire!' to have another go, be carried down on the fireman's back, or in the swing. This was a webbed seat, tied round the waist and attached to a gadget the girls referred to as a 'swing'. The fireman would turn a handle at great speed and they would swing to the ground. At their first fire practice, sometimes the girls would be too scared to do anything, but gradually the thrill and excitement got the better of them and they loved it. Some people would come to the fete just to watch this spectacular fire drill.

Marjorie remembers so many lovely things from her

childhood at Clacton. The charabanc outings on 15th August, in memory of John Groom's birthday; the picnics on the beach, the Easter walks and the autumn blackberrying. Like any normal child she was in innumerable scrapes. One features the annual visit of the dentist to the Homes. Rosebud was fifth in line, so waiting made things worse. Marjorie remembers clinging to the radiator, too frightened to go in, after hearing the screams and cries emanating from some poor victim in the room provided as a temporary surgery. As she herself explains it: 'No gas or cocaine in those days, just "open your mouth wider please," then Ouch! Out the tooth came.' Though she walked in meekly enough when her turn came, the look of triumph on the face of the attending nurse (whom she never liked!) when the dentist gave that fatal command to 'open her mouth a little wider' impelled her out of the chair in a bound and running like mad to the shelter of the fete ground. And there began a cat and mouse game to catch her among the tiered seats, which ended in her jumping in a hole covered by stinging nettles on a piece of waste ground. The Assistant Matron chasing her, refusing to be stung by nettles, gave in, so Marjorie won the day! The dentist went home, and since it was the weekend, Marjorie was given a reprieve until Monday. Painful though it was, she worked on that tooth all over the

Fire display at Fete Day, Clacton, 1905

weekend and managed to waggle it out, to the dentist's chagrin (and the nurse's!), triumphantly displaying an empty socket and no fear when that deadly command came to 'open your mouth a little wider.'

Once she had left school, there was training for domestic service. Mondays were for cleaning the long bay windows and scrubbing the linoleum flooring of the dormitories. On Tuesdays the girls' pinafores were washed and ironed. Marjorie explains:

'In those days it was a case of putting the heavy irons on the gas ring and using an iron holder. We would take them off the gas ring and spit on them to see if they were hot enough, or hold them near to our faces to gauge the temperature. Two irons were necessary, one on the gas ring while the other was in use, swapping them over when the first one grew too cold to be effective. It was a long and tedious job. Mother's bedroom and bathroom were cleaned on Wednesdays and there was the returned laundry to check and repair. Thursdays there was her sitting room to clean, and Fridays the kitchen to turn out, which meant the washing of all the crockery, cleaning the cutlery, polishing the big window and scrubbing the room length table, not forgetting the scrubbing and polishing of the floor and the blackleading jobs. The pantry was turned out on Saturdays. On Sundays only essential tasks were done. We had every afternoon off and fourpence per week (just under 2p) pocket money, but fourpence went a long way in those days.'

A new incentive came into Marjorie's life when she was discovered by long lost relatives, though she continued to spend the rest of her childhood at Clacton, through the 'reigns' of Matrons Phillips, Edwards, and much-loved Matron Langridge. But she went to live with her relations after completing her year of training for domestic service.

In 1939 the children's homes at Clacton seemed a long way from the war zones, but when a bomber, badly damaged with bombs still on board, made a forced landing nearby, the district was declared a danger zone.

The evacuation of the children had to be arranged. The children's homes which had seen so much activity, so much laughter, were soon to become silent. The well remembered fetes abruptly ended. No one anticipated, in those early days of the war, they would never return.

It was decided to try and keep the children together. Charles

O'Connor, having heard from Council member Mr. Ted Harman that a large house near Bridgnorth, belonging to Mrs. Leicester-Warren, seemed suitable, a visit was quickly arranged.

Davenport House was not being used by the Leicester-Warren family, who were concerned that it should be taken over for some good purpose, and the owner readily agreed to welcome the children.

Packing in a hurry and moving some 120 children was not an easy task. The younger ones went to the Edgware Estate in the care of Mrs. Corbett, a fine Canadian nursing sister, while the older ones made their way across country to Shropshire. Mrs. Kathleen Craft took charge of this group in a voluntary capacity. The babies later moved from Edgware to Farncote House near Wolverhampton. The children had always seemed so happy at Clacton and, once they had settled down in their new wartime homes, they were equally as happy.

The local village school could not cope with so many new children, so some classes were held at Davenport House. Mrs. Craft tackled her new responsibilities with great enthusiasm, while the children enjoyed the ponies and gardening and the rural situation. Talking about this years later, Mrs. Craft said this was one of the happiest times of her life.

Mrs. Lawson, in charge of the babies' work, was about to start a period of 26 years of devoted service and 40 years' interest in the work of John Grooms.

Back in Clacton, the old Homes had been taken over by the Army. During the evacuation of Dunkirk, many of those who had been rescued by the little boats, spent their first night back in Britain there. It must have been bliss to be able to sleep after the bombardment on the beaches. One war-worn soldier woke up and wondered where he was, having arrived late the night before. Doubtless there was some comment when, reporting for duty with another soldier the next morning, he announced: 'I'm Violet – and he's Forget-me-not!' No doubt the sick or wounded were in 'Daffodil' which had been in use as a Sanatorium for the children. It is interesting to note that John Groom once came to the Sanatorium to convalesce after a serious illness and it was there he met and married his second wife, Sister Ada, who helped him recover his health.

The war dragged on with all its 'blood, toil, tears and sweat.' Donations were received, children grew up, and the work of caring carried on despite all difficulties. Once the war was over, plans were made to get back to normal as speedily as possible. The Homes at Clacton were handed back by the Government, but needed to be repaired and restored to be suitable for children again. The babies were the first to return to Clacton, but it was decided not to reopen the other Homes, but rather to spread the children over a wider area and integrate them more into normal life.

The search for suitable premises was centred in Kent. Pilgrim House stood near Pilgrim's Way on the Westerham side of the Weald of Kent, about two miles from the delightful villages of Westerham and Chartwell. It was a marvellous place for the children with plenty of space, sports field, walled gardens and a wood. There was still a good bit of work to be done, but it offered great scope and the purchase was completed in 1946. Miss Boyd, who had taken over from Mrs. Craft at Davenport House, duly arrived with the children who were eventually put into Mrs. Everett's care who was matron for many years.

Shortly afterwards Cudham Hall, at Cudham in Kent, was found just a few miles from Pilgrim House. It was a delightful house situated in the centre of the village and, standing in its own

Matron Lawson at Cudham Babies' Home

landscaped garden, was a haven for the young pre-school children and babies, coming as they did from needy and broken homes. It had a large playroom, well equipped nursery school, paddling pool, lawns and a whole variety of other advantages. Mrs. Lawson, after a short period at Clacton with the babies, moved to this newly prepared house and 40 children were soon happily installed. Mrs. Lawson was a remarkable woman and, together with her staff, surrounded the children with love, care and affection. Her own daughter took her place amongst the children, but she did not look upon herself as any different, for her mother gave the same loving care to them all.

Charnwood, at Chislehurst, was purchased in 1956. This was a small family children's home, under the care of Mr. and Mrs. North in the first place, and later Mr. and Mrs. Cooke took over. This became a comfortable home for about 12 children, with the same kindly family spirit.

The Thorpe Bay children's home, which had been founded in 1910 as a Convalescent Home for disabled boys and girls, had been started by a determined young woman from Stamford Hill in North London who met young handicapped children in her Christian work. With help from her friends in the Congregational Church, she rented a house year by year for the summer months, and looked after her young visitors herself. Then a house was purchased at Thorpe Bay, Essex, and became Stamford Hill House, with Miss Holmes as its first Honorary Superintendent.

In 1951 John Grooms Association was invited to take over the work in this double-fronted house on the sea front. It was only a few yards from the beach and had accommodation for 16 children and 7 resident staff. Later 18 boys and girls were convalescing there. Girls up to sixteen years of age, and boys up to ten years were accepted, either disabled, delicate or needy. Some were received just to give the mothers a rest. In 1961 it was reported that nearly 200 children had visited the Home that year, drawn from many parts of the home counties.

But residential children's work was changing over the years and Grooms moved with the change. Fostering was proving better for the child than institutional care, because fostering resulted in the child being part of a natural family. Under the supervision of a social worker, babies in difficult circumstances were being kept at home, whereas in the past residential care would have been considered; it was the same for older children. There was also a greater demand for adoptions.

Consultation with various Government and local authorities resulted in the decision to put into effect a gradual closing down of children's residential work. It was not an easy decision to arrive at after such a history, especially in the light of the many thousands of children and young people who had been helped over a long period of years. However, John Grooms work for children was officially phased out with the closure of the Thorpe Bay Home in 1979, although the premises remained the property of the Association and were later to become the site of a whole new development. All the other homes were sold.

But even as the children's work was finishing for Grooms, the Association's work for disabled people was vastly on the increase. And to follow why this was so, we must first go back to the Edgware Estate.

Chapter 9

A TIME OF RAPID CHANGE

By 1965 everything was changing rapidly on the Edgware Estate. In its beginning, the Estate had been hailed as being of the highest standard. However, with the passage of time, expectations of disabled people were raised and governments introduced new legislation. Some of these rules meant that accommodation became 'sub-standard' overnight. At one time the **volume** of a room was critical and high ceilings became popular with architects. Later the floor area was the determining factor. A dormitory which slept a certain number of people had to have the numbers reduced. The cubicles at Edgware had been a compromise, allowing more residents in the house than if there had been individual rooms. There were tales of built-in cupboards being removed to meet the standards for floor areas and being replaced with a wardrobe taking up nearly as much room – far less suitable, but regarded as 'furniture' it did not reduce the floor space. Eventually each pair of semi-detached houses was converted into one and each girl was given a bed-sitter. Unfortunately, a side-effect of this was that subscribers being shown round commented that they themselves *'could not afford such luxury!'* – thus resulting in reduced donations. People just did not realise that the cost of complying with legislation for improvements far outweighed the finances available to achieve them.

The severely disabled young girls in wheelchairs, who had been accommodated in Lilac and Laburnum during my time at Grooms, had now been transferred to a new purpose-built house called 'Stoneyfields' at the top of the estate which was much more accessible. It housed twenty young residents and it was a highly desirable venture. Some had come from hospitals and chronic wards for the elderly, simply because there was nowhere else for them to go, and they could not be cared for in their own homes.

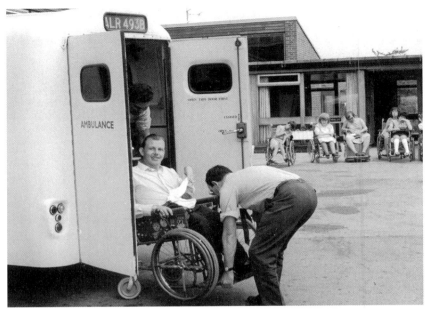

The first young man arrives at Edgware in 1970

The opening of Geoffrey Parker House

Jane, for instance, came straight from a special school and, being unable to return home, had been terrified of being sent to a long stay hospital unit. Instead, she found herself becoming a useful member of society and enjoying a full and satisfying life.

Geoffrey Parker, the Principal at that time, just before he retired saw the start of a house for severely handicapped young men which was eventually to be named after him. He then 'handed on the baton' to the Reverend Alfred Bell in the April of 1965, though he stayed on for the Centenary Celebrations in the October of that year. He and Mrs. Parker – known as 'Sister Ruth' because of her work with the Medical Mission – paid their usual visit to the houses at Christmas 1965, drove home, opened the garage doors and he died before he could return to the car to drive it into the garage. Geoffrey Parker House was officially opened by 'Sister Ruth' in 1970. The opening of this home was something of a landmark in the history of John Grooms, for young men, with background and plight similar to that of the young women, were being offered residential accommodation for the first time.

Matron Longley had taken early retirement through ill health and, during the interregnum period before Margaret Parnell took over, Sister Hall, who had been running the Nursing Home, deputised. Mrs Parnell became Matron in 1970. Like her predecessor, she had been a Missionary Nurse in Africa, where she had married John, who was priest in charge of the station. They had returned to a parish in Oxfordshire, but John had died and it was their thirteen year old son, seeing Grooms advertisement for a Matron in 'The Times', who had persuaded his mother to apply. She proved a very caring person, always ready to listen to staff or residents' problems. She put into practice the prayer, *'God grant me the sincerity to accept things I cannot change, the courage to change things I can, and the grace to know the difference.'* She stayed for two years and when she left, married a friend from early years, forming a useful partnership still helping others. She died tragically, trying without success to rescue friends staying with them when their cottage caught fire.

Mrs. Parnell was the last of the Matrons. Mrs. Sabina Bell, wife of the Principal, now acted as social worker. The loss of a Matron was not popular with the girls, who had always looked upon her as someone with whom they could share their problems but, in keeping with the times, Matrons were becoming a vanishing concept.

Life was also rapidly changing in the factory. It had been the aim of John Grooms from the beginning for the flower workers to be able to support themselves financially, although it had always been recognised that some would be unable to work as fast or long enough. Piecework had seemed a fair solution but, when the Social Security system was altered, Mr. Bell had long talks with those responsible which resulted in a subsidy to raise all low pay to a minimum level. This meant that those capable of earning more ended up with the same net income as someone able to earn only a little. It was hardly an incentive for those doing the best work to make the effort.

However, as girls aged and retired, flowers began stockpiling. Mr. Elmore had been employed as engineer in the Workroom by this time although, with the girls' interests so much at heart and being an extremely resourceful man, he was more like a 'Jack-of-all-Trades'. He invented a 'stocking-puller' for one, a special kind of 'helping-hand' for another and, because of their anxiety over their dwindling trade, obtained a promise from the Association that as long as they were able to work, flowers would continue to be manufactured. Such was his caring and the rapport between them, that talented Annie Small, working on stringing the Christmas tree lights, which entailed calling Mr. Elmore (he was known as 'Mr. Scratchit'!) for scratching off bits of glue or solder, could write:

> *'We've got a man who's always scratchin'*
> *but don't be alarmed, it''s nothing catchin' -*
> *He scratches gum from off the base*
> *Of bulbs that won't fit in the case.*
> *Mr. Elmore, will you scratch?*
> *This really has a nasty patch.*
> *It lights alright, but eee-by-gum*
> *to screw it hard, it hurts my thumb.'*

But he also had a great concern for the younger element, some of whom had come from very difficult backgrounds. Three young people in Dainesmead – Linda, Phyllis, and Jill – wanted desperately to work and would visit the factory daily just to watch the flower making. He went to see Mr. Parker and, eventually, these three were allowed into the factory to do artwork, enamelling and glass engraving, which Mr. Elmore supervised. It was the beginning of the Workrooms being known as the Craft (later, Activities) Centre, the whole of the south side of the factory being taken over as other enthusiasts joined them. The young men of Geoffrey Parker House were included, and they started up 'The Order of the Water Rats' – the 'rats' being the men, while the 'ratlings' were the ladies. They thought up the idea of inscribing their crest on mugs, so Mr. Elmore bought beer mugs by the carton, but it got to the point where they couldn't cope with demand. Frailty of their handicap kept many from working at too great a pace.

They also started to make a little lapel badge with a red rose on it as a symbol for Grooms. Lady Laing was involved, thrilled by the result, and wanted them in their thousands. They were made out of copper with the enamel rose embossed on. But once again the scheme fell through because those engaged on the work were not always robust enough to meet the demands being made on them.

But there was a wide range of other products, including cane chairs, cane-topped stools, coined bottle lamps and coins on plaques and flower pots. This was work they could do easily. If the coins got mixed up, it hardly mattered. I remember going round the Craft Centre and selecting, from a goodly collection, two framed etchings which are still my pride and joy!

A way opened for disabled people from outside the Estate to come to the Craft Centre just for the day. Their presence was welcome because it brought in a breath of fresh air to the estate. But unfortunately so many plans fell through because demands could not be met by stamina. Eventually, the Craft Centre was to change shape and become the Activities Centre and, later still, the Resources Centre, which was more leisurely and occupational in nature.

With the coming together of young disabled folk of both sexes, it was inevitable that romances would develop between them. One young man who had difficulty adjusting to Grooms, settled down as soon as romance blossomed and the couple were eventually married. Another young man was Brian Payne, who came to live at Geoffrey Parker House and who subsequently married Denise. Although severely physically handicapped, Brian had a very sharp and enquiring mind and, with the help of Possum Communication equipment connected to a typewriter (later a computer), he was able to edit and produce the Edgware Estate residents' house magazine as his main task at the Workrooms. 'Groonicle' was published two or three times a year

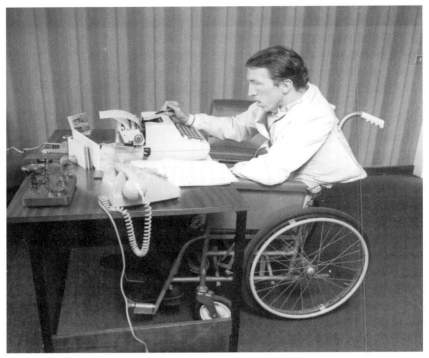

Brian editing 'Groonicle' magazine

for well over 10 years and had a wide readership both on and off the Estate, with a regular 'gossip' column by 'Alley-Cat' (a pseudonym) and contributions by other residents with literary talent.

To many, the thought of people in wheelchairs living by themselves, shopping, cooking and doing all the normal things about the home and getting married seemed just a wild dream. The vision John Grooms entertained was entirely different. They purchased a large old terraced house in North London and converted the ground floor to becoming fully wheelchair accessible by removing steps and adding wide doors and a spacious bathroom. A BBC radio producer was interested in this experiment in 1969 and broadcast an item about its purpose and aims. Shortly afterwards a telephone call was received suggesting that a young woman in hospital, who had been involved in a road accident and had lost the use of her legs, might be considered as the first tenant, as she had the will to try living independently.

This young woman was visited and it was discovered that, in her early years, she had been cared for in one of the Association's children's homes. So as soon as she was discharged from hospital she came to this adapted flat and quickly proved that independent living in a wheelchair was possible.

However, even in the late 1970's a disabled friend of mine requiring accommodation and approaching the local council was told: 'We don't cater for people like you!' That was still the attitude in general towards disabled people but, with legislation enforcing those who could work being given a chance of employment, medical science and rehabilitation centres making it possible for young people – and older! – to leave hospital and take

Charles O'Connor invites HRH The Duchess of Kent to open the Princess Crescent N4 flats – October 1973

up a new style of living in residential settings, attitudes had to change – Grooms were well in advance in setting the pace.

First of all they abandoned the ugly word 'cripple' from their vocabulary forever as in 1969 'John Groom's Crippleage' became 'John Grooms Association for the Disabled' – later, 'John Grooms Association for Disabled People'. Plans for a small group of flats were commissioned, born from the results of the experimental flat. The architect was C. Wycliffe Noble OBE and building was soon under way. This was in Finsbury Park at 9 Princess Crescent on the site of an old disused synagogue which was acquired for this purpose. All twelve flats were occupied almost before the

Tom and Jill Casey's wedding (John Keeble Church, Mill Hill)

builders had finished, such was the demand, and the Department of Environment awarded it a Certificate for Good Design. Each flat was designed to give independence and meet the special needs of tenants in wheelchairs, although a warden was appointed to deal with emergencies and provide any support that might be needed from time to time. By that time, too, Government policy having changed, some funding had become available through the Housing Corporation to provide Revenue Deficit Grant to subsidise rents in the early years.

Thus John Grooms Housing Association became a registered charity and Princess Crescent was officially opened in October 1973 by Her Royal Highness, the Duchess of Kent, accompanied by the then President of the Association, Lord Coggan, former Archbishop of Canterbury.

Jill, who has been mentioned as showing a lively interest in the Activities Centre, went to live at Princess Crescent. Although seriously handicapped by polio, she was a lively and attractive personality, and the first to lead in protests and get up petitions where she saw the need. Jill met Tom when he came to live at

Geoffrey Parker House. Tom had been born with only one leg. He found he could push a wheelchair quite a distance as it gave him support. He took Jill to discos. Romance developed and, despite staff misgivings, they married in John Keeble Church at Mill Hill. And this was when they moved to the Crescent. Mr.

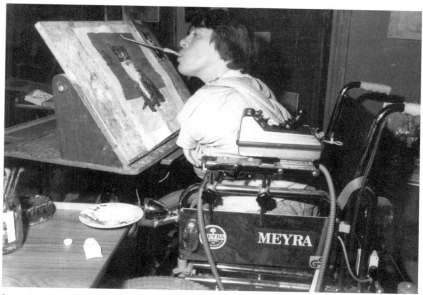

Lorraine Brasher painting by mouth (ATW)

Ken Eyers, as relief Warden, used to call and collect the rents for the flats. He comments that he would leave Jill until last, knowing she would have a cup of tea ready for him. He found her a good manager, always having her money ready for collection. One day she came to the door and greeted him with a huge smile. She had been able to cope with the bathroom all on her own for the first time in her life – at 26 years old! A Clos-o-Mat and an Electric hoist had made it possible.

Sadly, the marriage was of only short duration for Jill died of pneumonia, but not before, in Tom's testimony, she had given him 'the two best years of his life.'

In the late 1970s, Mrs. Hite, a voluntary worker, had started a dress making class for some of the ladies who were interested in this type of work and this was carried on in Stoneyfields House. It proved so popular that it prompted Charles Moore, who had now succeeded Mr. Alfred Bell as Director, to consider whether there were not other similar activities that might be added. A painting instructor was recruited and the painting classes started, which were eagerly anticipated by a number of residents including Lorraine Brasher who painted by holding the paint-brush in her mouth. Subsequently she joined the 'Mouth and Foot Artists' after she left John Grooms.

This activity became known as 'Alternatives To Work' (=ATW) because at the times these classes were being held other

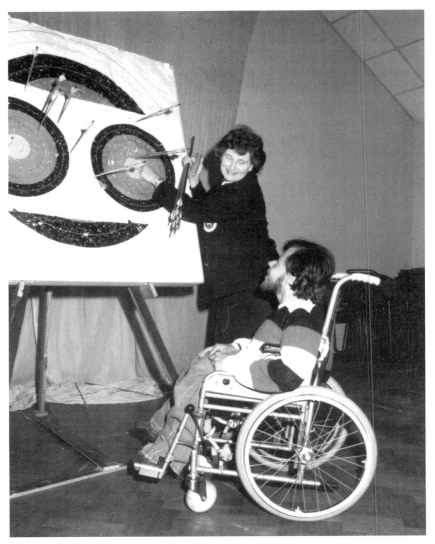

Archery class (ATW)

residents were working in the Craft Centre. Charles Moore encouraged Eric Elmore to expand the ATW by giving him a special brief to try and entice other residents to participate in them. Subsequent months saw the start of cookery, archery, woodwork, pottery and a number of other activities which were very popular. Also the regular swimming visits which the director personally made to Grooms' pool were taken over by an appointed instructor, with the hope of encouraging a wider use of the facility by the residents.

After consultation with an instructor at the local authority Flightways Centre, Mr. Elmore introduced a computer class and several BBC computers were purchased. These were quite quickly superseded by Amstrad machines and residents were encouraged to purchase their own computers with funds from sponsors. There was some concern at one stage as to whether sitting in front of the computer monitor for long was likely to cause epileptic fits and this was checked out with the Estate doctor, Dr. John Burke, who was able to give the necessary reassurance. Computing is still a very popular activity and the machines now being used are far more sophisticated than those early BBC computers. Resulting from contact with the Flightways unit, an instructor for a gardening class was obtained and this activity also proved popular with several residents.

Running parallel with these kind of changes were rapidly changing attitudes by and towards staff, not necessarily instigated by John Grooms. The impact of Social Service legislation introduced more structured and professional practices. For many years 'Housemothers' had been exactly what their name implied, many of them working with complete devotion and dedication without consideration of high salaries. However, conditions of employment have changed beyond all recognition within recent years and, due to severe disabilities, many residents now need high levels of personal care and the ratio of staff required to meet these needs has risen accordingly. Government registration rules also now require those in charge to be professionally qualified and Grooms has embarked on a training programme for **all** care staff. Perhaps there are those who look back with nostalgia to the informality and personal dedication shown by the former Housemothers, but there is little doubt that the true spirit of the Founder is still shown by staff employed in all aspects of the Association's work.

There has been a distinct change in attitudes towards

residents and within disabled people themselves. Long gone was the notion of privilege in being 'helped', however loving and kind that help may have been. Disabled people now had 'rights' that brought them equality with their able-bodied contemporaries. And forerunner to this vision, in 1973 Grooms began planning holidays.

Chapter 10

WISH YOU WERE HERE

During my time at John Grooms, preparing for the summer holiday had been like preparing for an assault course – though the girls with their marvellous adaptability seldom viewed it that way. To the younger element it was more of an adventure, the pivot round which all other affairs of the year circulated. In mid-July the factory and houses closed down completely for two weeks, leaving only office staff behind, while we all made our pilgrimages to the resorts of our own choosing.

Plans had to be made months ahead; in fact as the new year came in, so did the holiday dates. It was vitally necessary that arrangements should be made early, for suitable accommodation was limited. For some it mattered knowing beforehand how many stairs they had to climb, or whether there was a banister either side. You needed to be close to the sea when your walking was impaired and there was no one on hand to help you. Other difficulties, personal to each one, had to be sorted out before making a booking. It was all done by letters – telephoning was not everyone's means of communication in those days.

Washing (no washing machines!), ironing, packing, all had to be started days beforehand. If you were disabled you couldn't cope with travelling and luggage. The week before departure day, the hall of the house resembled a main line goods depot with all its neatly sewn hessian covered suitcases – a well tried protection against damage – waiting for collection by British Rail. Once the luggage had gone there was nothing more to do than wait for Saturday and pray that the weather would be kind and that one's luggage would not get lost but be there on one's arrival.

There were many kind friends from the Mill Hill churches who used their cars as a taxi service getting the girls to the main line stations or coach depots. Ethel Lee was a survivor from

Sekforde Street, and to see her depart that Saturday morning was an experience never to be repeated! No wonder she preferred to hire her own taxi! Luggage spilled from every corner, while perched on top of all was the bulky three-wheeler self-propelling chair that went everywhere with her. Finally, Ethel herself would emerge on her two sticks, (dressed in clothes I strongly suspect had survived Sekforde Street also for, like Doris mentioned in a previous chapter, Ethel never discarded anything) and majestically approached her awaiting carriage.

Travelling by train had its perks; if you did not want to run the risk of not finding a seat, you could write beforehand to the main line station and book one. Then on the day of departure you would find yourself escaping the queue and being escorted like royalty by the station master in his braided cap of authority to – not a seat – but a whole first class compartment especially reserved for you and your friend! There it was – the large label on the window announcing: 'Reserved for Miss....... and Companion.' You had the privilege of refusing access to anyone else. And all for a mere shilling each (5p) on top of your normal second class fare!

Of course, this was only if you were not totally confined to a wheelchair. If you were, you were less fortunate and travelled in the guard's van, half price admittedly, but amongst all the other freight. My disabled friend, travelling in her self-propelling chair, once found herself sharing space with a Great Dane, who was more perturbed than she was when the motion of the train jolted her inch by inch towards the animal despite her brakes being on!

Eventually a seat was removed in a first class compartment so that the wheelchair could be wheeled into its place. But it was useless if the connecting corridor to the compartment was too narrow for the wheelchair to pass through. So, when motor chairs supplied by the Ministry began being available to those competent to drive them, it proved a great blessing to be able to drive to one's holiday destination without hassle.

Matron Longley would work inexhaustibly trying to fix holidays for girls who were unable, or finding difficulty, in booking up for themselves. Specialised guide books began coming on to the market during my latter years at Grooms, but in those days the information proved inadequate. 'No steps to entrance. Everything on ground floor', reads the blurb. Fine – but no mention about the small steps down to the dining room! This may be hardly noticeable to the able-bodied, but with no rail to cling on to a real hazard to someone in callipers, and a disaster to anyone trying to manipulate themselves in a wheelchair. 'Bathroom same floor as bedroom' – yes – if you forget the two steps mid-landing that level it! And without a hoist how do you manage to transfer from wheelchair to a bed which is not of the same height!

These difficulties were not just the prerogative of the John Grooms' ladies. There were a whole lot more disabled people among the general public for which something needed to be done.

Prompted by this need, Charles O'Connor, Association Secretary between the years 1944 – 1976, began searching the countryside for a suitable building that could be converted to the holiday needs of disabled people. When he spotted it, he knew immediately this was 'it' – though it was not up for sale, no inkling that it was likely to be, nor did he know the proprietors. Nevertheless, strongly urged from within, he went back to his office and wrote to the proprietors telling them that, if they were thinking of selling, Grooms was interested.

There would have been every reason to believe that he had been mistaken in his inner guidance when no answer came. Then, miraculously, the reply came some time later. It appeared that the proprietors, thinking the letter was an appeal for a subscription had, as was their custom, put it aside for consideration during the winter months. They were very interested in Mr. O'Connor's proposal and, in due course, sold the building to Grooms for £43,000. And that was the beginning of the Promenade Hotel at Minehead. It stands in a delightful position on the sea front, with extensive views over sea and harbour, and nestling within the shadow of lovely North Hill. Neither did Grooms have to worry about money for the purchase. An appeal for the venture brought a response in the way of a cheque from an anonymous donor covering the whole amount! – truly demonstrating this was a Godly concern.

Of course, there had to be many alterations: ramps to replace steps, a lift that could accommodate wheelchairs – bathrooms likewise – widening of corridors and bedrooms, and installing of electric hoists and alarm system. By Spring 1976 renovations were completed and the hotel was open for business.

The following year, a disabled friend and myself spent a holiday there. Our first agreeable surprise was meeting up again with Mr. Ken Eyres and his wife, Jo. We had last seen them ten years ago when he had been assistant to Mr. Parker on the

Promenade Hotel, Minehead, Somerset

Edgware Estate. Now we discovered he had been appointed as manager of the Promenade Hotel.

We have since visited this hotel fourteen times, and over that period a worsening of my friend's disability surely demonstrates not only how adaptable to disabled needs this hotel has proved, but also how successful. There is such a pleasant atmosphere that during the whole of our stay we feel as though we are living on a higher plane. In a literal sense we are on a 'higher plane' in the hotel's mini-bus (specially adapted to accommodate wheelchairs with their occupants sitting in them) than is possible in a car during the afternoon tours of the countryside. Raised above those high West Country hedges, road winding up and up, it requires little imagination to visualise outlaws having the run of that vast hilly territory, trees rising from ugly roots, twisted and gnarled, dwarfing the road beneath which in earlier times would have been unmade and a 'boggy slough cake' as R.D. Blackmore colourfully describes it.

Our kindly driver, knowing the locality well, cares enough to take us along many a hitherto unexplored byway that will give us the most colourful journey. We are refreshed by views of much glorious undulating landscape dotted with sheep, cows and a few horses. Another incentive for relaxing is the colourful Blenheim Gardens close by and the stillness of the centuries old harbour in the evening light. Or, at an appropriate time in the evening, you can watch wild rabbits running free where country and sea meet at the base of North Hill.

Shops are within easy walking distance and, for some mornings, there are volunteer 'pushers' for those in wheelchairs requiring their services. Often we would come back from our shopping spree laden, my friend in her wheelchair hidden under packages, enjoying an outing not so easily managed at home. Sunday mornings would find us in the local Methodist church, which is only a short distance from the hotel and all on the level. It is so easy of access that we would find ourselves one in a queue of wheelchairs along the aisle.

Once, one thing puzzled my friend. Why couldn't she see the flashing beam of the lighthouse from her bed as she had done in other years? A slight strain on her arms transferring from wheelchair to bed told her that the blocks on which the bed was resting could have been a fraction higher. But she only told the manager the night before we were going home.

'Now she tells me,' Mr. Eyres groaned, wondering why his efforts to urge us at the very beginning of our holiday to ask for anything for our comfort should have fallen on such deaf ears! For that is the secret of the Promenade's success. Nothing is too much trouble for the staff. Mr. and Mrs. Eyres will have retired by the time this book comes into print, but they are leaving behind a sure pattern of management and caring that cannot be surpassed since it is based on the same Christian empathy that inspired John Groom in the beginning.

Within three years of opening, the Promenade Hotel became so heavily booked that, when the former Chief Coastguard's cottage fell vacant on the sea front and only a few yards from the hotel, it was purchased, adapted and modernised to house the 'overflow'. There were three bedrooms facing the sea on the ground floor and accommodation for accompanying able-bodied friends or family on the floor above. It was a delightful extension to the main building. This has now closed, but further improvements have been made in the hotel and each room has now been fitted with its own toilet and shower en suite.

With the success of the Promenade Hotel and the many requests for holiday accommodation that were not being met from any other source, a fresh search was undertaken by Grooms. It was the then Chairman, Mr. Frank Willows and Mr. O'Connor (by now retired as Secretary), who discovered the West Shore Hotel, Llandudno, and it was purchased in 1978. Of course there had to be major conversions and the original hotel was doubled in size by the extensions. It is a bigger hotel than the Promenade and proved a more costly venture, but was considerably helped by a grant from the European Economic Commission who, interested when approached, saw this as a pilot scheme that might entice European wheelchairs users to visit this country, and also encourage other EEC countries to carry out similar projects.

West Shore Hotel, Llandudno, North Wales

This hotel, situated on the West Shore of Llandudno, North Wales, stands right on the sea front at the foot of the Great Orme, a rocky promontory reaching 400 ft above sea level. Run on the same principles as the Promenade, it has proved highly successful, and was initially the only wheelchair-accessible hotel in Llandudno. At first the local Hoteliers Association were hostile, but they came round to being very supportive when it was realised Grooms only concern was helping disabled people and not a desire to steal their trade from them. Now Grooms are delighted that many other hotels in the town have been made 'wheelchair friendly' as a result of their pioneering and open spirit.

Both the West Shore Hotel and the Promenade Hotel were awarded Certificates of Merit by the British Tourist Authority during the International Year of Disabled People in 1981. In addition, the Welsh Tourist Board awarded West Shore Hotel a special medal designed and made by the Welsh Royal Mint.

After that, Grooms holidays just 'snowballed'. Not every disabled person wants an hotel-type holiday. Some require something cheaper they can share with the whole family and prefer doing their own catering. Grooms recognised this need and in 1979 their Holiday Committee travelled to Didcot to see the prototype fixed site caravan which had been adapted to the needs of disabled people by the Donnington Company, owned by a disabled entrepreneur. The Committee were so impressed they ordered one of the mobile homes on the spot and sited it on the Naish Caravan Park near Bournemouth. This was the first of a series of caravans to be sited in various holiday locations throughout England and Wales over the following four or five years.

My disabled friend and myself decided, one year, to sample this type of holiday. We chose Sandford Park, which is a natural park in fifty acres of heathland situated between Ware and Bournemouth and within easy access of both. The caravan was forty feet in length and ten feet wide, well ramped for entry and exit and, since it was meant to accommodate six people, we luxuriated in the room space. Our neighbouring van was the counterpart of ours but owned by the Spina Bifida Association. All other caravans and chalets on the site were occupied by able-bodied holidaymakers, and we enjoyed being part of them, watching children in the paddling pool, or swimmers in the adult one. It was easy to shop in the camp supermarket or, if we did not want to cook, we could enjoy a meal in the cafeteria or restaurant on the site. There were all the other amenities of a holiday site to sample and, if the only desire was to relax quietly, there was one's own small patch of grass surrounding the van where you could bask in the sunshine. This caravan has now been exchanged for something even better – a pinelog luxury chalet, fully wheelchair-accessible and still sleeping six people.

So many disabled people had been disappointed in the past with facilities which did not match up to the owners' descriptions that Grooms, networking with two or three local organisations for disabled people, acquired two chalets and two caravans with funds provided by the local groups who were then given priority in booking for the first part of each season.

A further step came when a bungalow at Wroxham, in the heart of the Norfolk Broads, was presented and opened on 8th

Rockley Park Chalet, near Poole, Dorset

Nationwide bungalow, Ambleside, Cumbria

May 1981. It was a gift from Mrs. Hill, whose husband spent thirty years in a wheelchair, a victim of multiple sclerosis. When offering this property to Grooms, Mrs. Hill said her husband – who had a great compassion for other people's troubles and difficulties – would have been gratified to know it was going to be put to good use for other disabled people. Certainly it has proved popular and been well used over the years. However, although the original building has had to be demolished because of recurring dampness problems, it has recently been replaced by four flats, two being for holiday use and two for residential, which have been built on the same site. Mrs. Hill and her family later gave the Association another holiday bungalow at Clacton-on-Sea and this, together with a further acquisition at Ambleside in the Lake District, has proved very popular with disabled holidaymakers. In spite of the extra initial cost, a particular advantage of these bungalows is their relative durability, for the caravans have necessarily to be replaced after about ten years.

One of our less successful ventures was in the early 1980's when mobile caravan holidays were becoming very popular. Grooms acquired such a vehicle which had been specially adapted to make it wheelchair accessible with a Ratcliffe tail-lift. It was fitted out to suit a family of four with one wheelchair user, and hired out for periods of one or two weeks. It was much in demand, but unfortunately its popularity was rather short-lived as in the second season, when a last minute booking was accepted, the hirer was subsequently discovered to have used bogus credentials, taken the motor caravan to the Continent and promptly disappeared with it! The last Grooms heard of this vehicle was that it had been sighted in the south of France but the police never traced it. So that chapter closed with a total loss insurance claim and it was decided regretfully not to replace the vehicle as there was no way of preventing it falling into unscrupulous hands again!

London was not left out of Grooms holiday planning. In 1976 a holiday flat was opened in the Finsbury Park complex. It was self-catering, with two bedrooms and could sleep six. Many have expressed their appreciation at being able to have a carefree holiday in reasonably priced suitable accommodation, close to shops and less than five miles from central London. Many wheelchair visitors have included Americans, Australians, some from New Zealand and several from Europe.

And after a lot of abortive work, an arrangement was

Jane Hodge Hotel swimming pool, Trerhyngyll, South Wales

eventually reached with the Copthorne Tara Hotel, at their cost, for adapting twelve rooms to the requirement of disabled guests to the design recommended by Charles Moore and his team at the London Hotel for Disabled People organisation. Disabled visitors desiring to use the Tara facilities are invited to join the London Visitors Club and this then entitles them to a huge discount off the normal commercial rate. It is a very popular facility and is still ongoing, although now managed and operated by the independent 'Holiday Care Service' charity.

Another venture of which Grooms is very proud is the Jane Hodge Hotel. This new purpose-built hotel is situated in quiet Trerhyngyll surrounded by the glorious countryside within the Vale of Glamorgan. The original building standing on this site, founded by Sir Julian Hodge and named after his mother, was demolished in 1989. It was a centre designed to provide holidays for thalidomide children in dormitory accommodation and, although many youngsters have enjoyed holidays there over the years, times have changed and the facilities were in great need of upgrading. It was also facing heavy financial losses, so Grooms were invited by Sir Julian and the Hodge Foundation to take over the site and rebuild and organise it in their own way for the benefit of disabled people generally. Within their plans Grooms also had in mind the needs of the carer who can become exhausted looking after a severely disabled person day and night.

Quickly realising that the existing buildings were totally inadequate by present standards, they decided to demolish them all and – with the aid of a forty-five per cent European Community (ERDF) grant of its total cost (which, including a subsequent extension, amounted to over £2.7 million) – built a new hotel altogether, which was officially opened on 19th July 1991 by Viscount Tonypandy. Funds poured in so miraculously – the Welsh Tourist Board, alone, donated £200,000 – that, once again, the whole project seemed divinely guided.

The hotel can accommodate 54 people in all (this includes a caring friend or family a disabled guest may bring with them). Providing 'in house' care has not proved economically viable, but this has been overcome by operating the care service on an agency basis, though there are also some Community Service Volunteers who live in from two to six months and who receive only pocket money. Three carers are on day shift all the time, two at night. I was very conscious of loving concern towards the disabled people all about me in my brief stay at the hotel for research for this book. The kind, warm personality of Glenda Thomas, the manageress, deceptively hides the skill that must be required to run this complex, for the service is second to none. The hotel can be used for conferences, group holidays, special interest weeks and very many indoor activities, including a warm swimming pool, jacuzzi and sauna.

In fact, because of its unique range of features and services, the Jane Hodge Hotel has already won several awards and is one of the first hotels to be given the national accessibility symbol, 'Tourism for All'. It has also been named Regional Winner of the European Commission Initiative for providing the most comprehensive facilities for disabled visitors.

Facilities are open to the public at cost and integration with the disabled guests is encouraged, but there is every facility for being alone if preferred. Each room opens out on to its own portion of ground. One of the delights I experienced was hearing the country sounds of an adjacent farm first thing in the morning. I was thinking how ideal the setting could prove for a newly disabled person trying to adjust to life or recovering after illness, when I was approached by a guest who explained how he had brought along a relative just recovering from a stroke and how tremendously the holiday had helped.

Conference type disabled groups, especially for young people, are encouraged. Recently, one group came from Belgium. Tanni Gray, Gold Medallist for the Paraplegic Olympics, lives in Cardiff and is pleased to use the gym for her training. And there has even been romance. Two people have met and married, holding their wedding breakfast and honeymooning at the hotel.

However, it must be pointed out that because of its idyllic position you need a car, or the mini-bus to travel far afield. The mini-bus runs trips into Cardiff for shopping, or will pick guests up at Cardiff Station or Airport. Ronnie Ambler both drives and maintains the bus and I shall long remember the trip he took us on to view the Rhondda Valley from high up in the hills. It was a glorious sunny morning, and it was no trouble for him and his kindly helpers to lift out the disabled visitors so they could share in the lovely view. One guest, Hazel Martin, came from Geoffrey Parker House on the John Grooms Edgware Estate. She is so severely disabled, she practically reclines in her wheelchair. She could enjoy the view as much as I could, while being lovingly fed with ice cream by one of the carers. Bless you, Hazel, for leaving me with such a happy memory – and for Grooms, forerunner in making such integration possible.

So, for the holiday welfare of disabled people, tentacles have widely spread from the spearhead of Minehead, that first hotel brought into being through the almost visionary influence of Charles O'Connor, into an ever expanding future of holidays both at home and abroad.

Chapter 11

'IT'S MY TURN TO USE THE WHEELCHAIR'

By far the greater sector of recent growth in the Association lies within housing. John Groom, walking the streets of London in the nineteenth century was so appalled by what he saw in the needs of disabled people, he just had to do something about it. He was way ahead of his time, working hard to establish that disabled people were people with the same hopes and desires that we all have. They had a right to a home, a job and an income, and a right to be a normal part of society. Today we call it integration.

John Groom's only knowledge of modern transport were the trains and the beginnings of the motor car. What would he have thought of the appalling accidents that have disabled myriads of people today as a result of this rapidly advancing technology in travel? There may not be the same basic need for food, clothing and shelter for disabled people as there was in his time, but the inner needs penetrate far, far, deeper. In a society brought up to value independence as a 'right', these profound inner hurts still exist even though the general public walking the streets cannot possibly see them. There are infinitely more disabled people today than there were in John's time for, with the advance of medical science and provision, people are now surviving serious road accidents and other hazards. They yearn to live as near normal a life as possible.

Also, when a degenerative disease or illness sets in, it should no longer be necessary for a person to be sent to an institution or hospital. With an individually sensitively designed housing unit and care package, they could live independently and fully. Yet thousands of young people are living in unsuitable residential establishments, **and in all cases living as near normal a life as possible means maintaining control of your life and**

doing as much for yourself as you are capable of – not having it done for you.

Picture it! You have been involved in a car accident while on your way to begin a post graduate course in social work. You are unconscious for four and a half months, and when you do rally you are brain damaged. At twenty-four years of age you find yourself just like a baby, having to learn to think, move and talk all over again. And with tremendous courage you do this, and make sufficient progress even to train for some kind of employment. But there is nowhere suitable for you to live. Do you deserve to come to such a dead end in your quest for as near normal a life as possible? In this true instance, Grooms were able to give incentive to this young woman's life by providing her with a suitable flat.

Wheelchair user Yvonne and her able-bodied friend decided to go on holiday abroad. Arriving at the airline check-in, the woman at the desk looked right down on Yvonne and enquired which of the two was disabled! One must give this questioning lady the benefit of going on a roundabout and inane way of discovering the name of the disabled person! Certainly she deserved the smart answer she received: 'She is,' said Yvonne, pointing to the friend standing beside her. 'But it's my turn to use the wheelchair!'

There is more subtlety in that humour than realised, for the only way to be a Good Samaritan to disabled people is to put oneself in another's wheelchair! In the mid 1980's Grooms encouraged this attitude by running a competition for children under sixteen under the title: 'How An Accident Changed My Life'. The winner, Dawn Boles of Stanwell, fourteen at the time, showed remarkable insight. She wrote:

> 'I looked up into the sky. It was pure light blue. There were a few white fluffy clouds which just finished it off. Two bluebirds were chirping excitedly in the air. In fact, everything was perfect. That is, except me. Not that I resented anybody, even myself, for it. It was nobody's fault. Accidents do happen. And this one did.
>
> When the doctor told me I had lost the use of my legs, I didn't know what to think. And right now, I still don't. It's like somebody coming to you and saying – "How would you like to change your life? Start all over again?" – But this time it's worse.
>
> Just then my mum called me: "Dawn, your dinner's ready!"
>
> Turning round in my wheelchair, I was faced by my first major problem – the step.

There was no way my wheelchair could get up it and my mum had forgotten. Mind you, I don't blame her. Only a few weeks ago I was plain normal Dawn Boles – but all that's changed. I thought to myself, "God, don't let it be like this all the time. I want to be independent, not like this."

My mum put down the spaghetti saucepan. "The step," she mumbled, "Of course!"

She came into the garden. "I'm sorry about that, Dawn," she said. "I completely forgot." She lifted me into the kitchen and wheeled me to the table. Elaine, my sister, was looking very thoughtful. I suppose it's hard for a seventeen-year-old girl to accept that she's got a disabled sister. My mum was quiet too. Usually at dinner time we're all chatting away happily. My heart was pounding heavily. I could almost tell what they were thinking about. It was very hard for my mum to come to terms with this accident. You see, three years ago my dad had died of an incurable disease. The disease was Leukaemia. And now this. People were so sympathetic and kind when they first heard about my disabilities. But you see, being like that doesn't seem to help. You don't want people to say "Ah, poor Dawn, so young, too....." etc., but you want them to treat you normally – as though it doesn't matter that you haven't got legs – but it does. To them, you're different, you see. Well, maybe in looks but not in yourself. People don't realise that I don't need all the sympathy and pity – but my dad did. It was hard for people to see that he was ill – so ill that he was dying upwards. Unless you look ill or different they just don't understand.

Interrupting my thoughts, my mum got up – "Er, Dawn, I didn't tell you, but Dr. Taylor came to see how you are progressing today – I told him you were coping with the wheelchair and getting…"

"Why?" I asked.

She looked into my saddened face – "What do you mean?"

"Why didn't you let me tell him? I wish Mum, that you and everyone out there in that world could understand I'm still *me* and I'm still capable of thinking for myself!"

I turned my wheelchair and left the room. As I did so a tear fell on to my lap, and for a small moment I wished I could get up and run – run far, far away...'

The aim of John Grooms Housing Association is to give disabled people who feel like that somewhere to run to – and not too far away!

1981 proved an important turning point in breaking down barriers between able and disabled people and gaining better insights on many problems. The Libyan representative to the

International Year of Disabled People (IYDP) symbol 1981

United Nations put forward a suggestion to the General Assembly that this should be a special year to focus attention on disability issues. The idea received international support with Great Britain as co-sponsor. Thus the International Year of Disabled People (IYDP) 1981 was born.

Four simple aims were adopted:

> Increasing awareness of the needs, abilities and aspirations of disabled people.
> The participation, equality and integration of disabled people within society.
> The prevention of disability.
> More positive attitudes towards disabled people.

The 'logo' agreed upon was simple. It represented two people holding hands in solidarity and support of each other. Put simply, 'not being left out.'

Activity began across the world. Here in the UK a main committee was formed with The Prince of Wales as Patron and Lord Snowdon as President. From the very start there was clear determination that there should be action not just talk. Some fourteen working groups were formed covering a whole range of important aspects such as Relationships, Housing, Employment, Technology, Sport, Information, Access and Attitudes, to name about half of them. Many local groups were formed and just about all committees drew in disabled people as active members. The Prime Minister, the Rt Hon Mrs Margaret Thatcher, held a reception at 10 Downing Street, the Prince of Wales called together business men, a special garden party was held at Buckingham Palace, and the Archbishop of Canterbury did the same at Lambeth Palace. The Post Office issued four special stamps and there were many special radio and television programmes transmitted by all stations.

There was a vast amount of activity throughout the UK, but what was most impressive was the desire to pool resources locally and nationally, to work together in partnership and to see real long term results. Yet it also shone out once more how ahead of his time John Groom had been, for many of the IYDP ideals had been his in the nineteenth century.

MP's are always busy people, particularly so when they happen to be Prime Minister. Although the Edgware estate fell just outside Mrs Thatcher's parliamentary constituency area, Grooms' director Charles Moore felt justified in inviting her to make a personal visit to the estate, especially in IYDP. Mrs Thatcher's acceptance started an interest that extended over the following few years and she was pleased to visit to present an ambulance purchased from the proceeds of the Barnet Mayoral appeal. She later opened two housing developments completed in Stoneyfields Lane and on the adjacent 'backland', which had been cultivated during the 'Dig for Victory' campaign in World War II.

An imaginative mobile exhibition was designed and commissioned by Grooms Association for IYDP and was aptly named 'The Groomsmobile – the able disabled exhibition.' This was launched at Guildhall in London by the Rt Hon The Lord Mayor of London and the Minister of State for Disabled People, Mr Hugh Rossi MP, who both showed a close and practical interest in all the exhibits and experiences which 'Groomsmobile' offered.

No-one could fail to see the rainbow coloured 40ft. of van and trailer packed with equipment as it travelled thousands of miles throughout the UK visiting schools, youth organisations, clubs and groups of all kinds. It appeared in public car parks, town halls, and even on seaside promenades and always had a good reception. Very much a 'hands on' approach, the aim of the

The Groomsmobile exhibition 1981

exhibition was to give visitors an experience of disability and the way in which disabled people can be integrated into normal living. Visitors were both amazed and fascinated by the huge range of equipment which could make life easier for people with a disability. Not many people had seen gadgets that enabled a person who could not see to tell when his/her cup was full of hot tea, or when it started to rain so that the drying washing could be brought in. Also exhibited were alarms for people who cannot hear, sophisticated equipment to help people with speech difficulties and simple equipment to enable people to peel a potato with one hand, or carry a cup of tea if you are unsteady on your feet. If visitors were willing, they would be offered a temporary handicap – say losing an arm – one arm would be secured behind the back and a simple everyday task would be suggested, such as opening a letter. Solutions to all the problems were on hand in the exhibition.

The second part of the exhibition was a series of photographs showing disabled people active in every aspect of normal life. Photographs of well known people who overcame their disabilities and who the world recognised for their abilities. These included Lord Nelson (one eye and one arm), a great director of battles at sea; Douglas Bader, the second world war legless fighter pilot; Helen Keller (without sight or hearing) who did such great work in her field. Roosevelt, President of the USA used a wheelchair. Then there were Flanders and Swann of 'Mud, Mud, Glorious Mud' fame – do you know which one was in a wheelchair?

Last stop in the 'Groomsmobile' was to try the exciting wheelchair obstacle course. Literally 'putting oneself in another's wheelchair!' Visitors would be given a wheelchair and invited to tackle the course of ramps, doors only just wide enough to allow a wheelchair through, the problems of small (normal) toilets or steps and things too high or too low – the problem of a world built for people who walk. Visitors who did the course are not expected to forget the experience – they will also have some understanding of what is needed. The Minister for Disabled People had a go and commended it on the BBC and the exhibition was featured on local and national programmes.

The demand for the Exhibition was considerable and all the requests could not be met in IYDP. The Association maintained the Exhibition for three years, despite the fact that it was designed for just a year's use, until it was worn out by the use of thousands of visitors. For some six million disabled people 1981 was a watershed. Radical thinking was taking place; charities, organisations and local authorities were pulling together, disabled people were being involved and treated as 'able' people. Partnership and participation was happening and so much good came from the year which is still ongoing and showing results years later.

And John Grooms has kept faith with the international aspect of the project. Over recent years the Association has developed a relationship with the Africa Inland Mission (AIM) through Allan Plumpton who took over from Charles O'Connor as Association Secretary in 1976 and is Honorary Treasurer to the Mission. This Christian missionary society, as its name suggests, is active across Central and East Africa, working in partnership with the Africa Inland Church (AIC), spreading the Gospel and bringing practical help to those most in need. John Grooms has supplied the AIC Child Care Centre in Kajiado, Kenya, with material and specialist equipment for its disabled children. Although our contributions are small, they make a real difference in Africa, as a letter from Miss Georgie Orme, AIM missionary responsible for the Centre in Kajiado reveals.

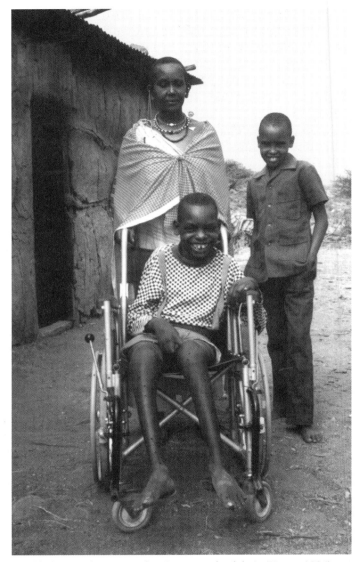

Disabled Masai boy in a John Grooms wheelchair (Kenya 1994)

She writes:

'The timing and the sovereignty of God never cease to thrill me. He has continued to supply everything we need, and sometimes He does it in quite an extraordinary way.

I was in Nairobi in March, and was handed a box which had been sent to us. Inside were four pairs of the smallest white

142

orthopaedic boots, sizes 00 and 0. They were Dennis Browne splint-boots, which are used as an effective treatment for club-feet in children. We had no such children at the Mission at the time, so I wondered when I would ever use them.

The very next morning a new patient arrived in my office. A Masai woman appeared at my desk, clutching a one-month old baby with – yes, you have guessed it – congenital club feet! She could only have worn the smallest Dennis Browne splint-boots size 00!

My mind strayed straight to Isaiah, and to the Lord's words:

"Before they call, I will answer. And while they are still speaking, I will hear." '

Stories like this are not uncommon. The work of Christian organisations in Africa can sometimes appear to the outside world to be overshadowed by the nihilism and despair that accompanies reports on droughts, plagues, famine and war. But faith is still alive, and God answers prayer.

Another aspect of Grooms co-operation abroad with other agencies is their work in conjunction with the Centre for the Rehabilitation for the Paralysed (CRP) in Bangladesh, the only centre in the country coping with the special medical needs of those with spinal injuries. A new hundred bedded hospital has been built with small purpose-built wards to replace the former dilapidated tin roof affair.

The Centre was set up in 1979 by Valerie Taylor OBE, a British physiotherapist. Grooms connection began after Lord Swinfen, Grooms Executive Officer, in order to promote fund-raising revived the custom of sending emblem roses to Embassies all over the world. In 1991 he received a reply from Colin Imray, High Commissioner in Bangladesh, saying that he would like roses for the Queen's birthday garden party that he would be giving. There would be 400 guests.

Lord Swinfen explains: 'When the roses were sent to him I wrote and asked if he would have lunch with me and tell me about disability in Bangladesh, which he did when next home on leave. He then kindly invited my wife and me to stay with the High Commissioner in Dhaka. We gladly accepted as we had always wanted to go to India, and so went there on holiday and on to Bangladesh in January 1992. We investigated various organisations in Bangladesh helping disabled people and decided that we could work with the Centre for the Rehabilitation of the Paralysed (CRP). Its ethos of trying to make disabled people independent is the same as John Grooms.'

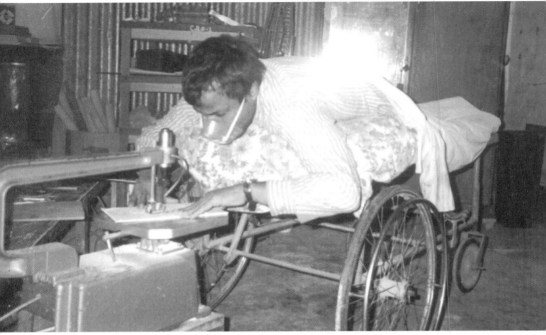

An enterprising Bangladeshi man working a jigsaw at CRP (1995)

Lord Swinfen visited Bangladesh again the following year to discuss various aspects of their work and in the October of 1993 sent Richard Hale and Trevor Jones to make detailed professional assessments. Plans were made for sending others out later. Stephen and Maggie Muldoon have both worked for Grooms in the UK and late in 1995 embarked on an innovative nurse training programme at CRP in Dhaka, training local staff on how to care for and help with the rehabilitation of those with spinal and other disabling injuries at the Centre.

Many of the spinal injuries are caused by the tradition in Bangladesh of carrying heavy loads on the head. 'For workers who are paid by the amount they can carry, the temptation to be over-loaded is great,' comments Lord Swinfen. 'Trip on the uneven roads and pathways with a pile of bricks on your head and your neck breaks. Often accidents occur to youngsters picking fruit from high trees and falling. It's often as simple as that. Following such injuries there are few facilities; wheelchairs are hard to come by and, for women especially, the situation is dire. Women who cannot work (or bear children) are of small value in Bangladesh society. They receive little care, often suffering secondary symptoms such as life-threatening pressure sores or infections.'

Nonetheless they are a brave people who believe in ability, not disability. Like Madhab, who broke his neck in a fall when he was fourteen. At CRP he discovered his talent to paint, and his art has sold worldwide. Manwar Hossain had a motor-cycle accident

Wheelchair basketball in Bangladesh (1995)

in which his son died and he fractured his skull and neck. He was completely paralysed. At CRP he learnt to hope, to stand, and finally to walk again – without even a stick. He now teaches young patients to read and write. Mamtaz Begum of Jessore suffered serious injury to the spinal cord as a result of a bus accident. 'I lost all hope but now I find I can get back to my school where I teach and lead a normal life,' she said, tears of relief rolling down her cheeks.

'Nowhere else have I seen wheelchair-accessible cattle and goat houses, or wheelchair-mobile people being taught duck, chicken and fish farming.' Lord Swinfen remarks. 'It was heart-warming to see the hope and renewed purpose in life this inspired.'

Neither does the Centre's involvement with patients end the moment they leave. In a vehicle specially adapted for disabled drivers, a social worker heads an outreach team on weekly visits to former patients, often to distant rural areas.

Earlier there were other small overseas ventures. In Pakistan, money and materials were made available for locally made callipers to be supplied to polio children. It is a great encouragement to know that some are now walking again. A small amount of much needed equipment was sent to Zambia to meet the needs of a few disabled people who live some 500 miles from the shops. And Grooms even felt able to support an appeal for two special three-wheeled cycles for disabled youngsters in India to enable them simply to get around.

★   ★   ★   ★

Charles Moore, who was at that time Assistant Secretary and subsequently became the first Director of the Association, proved to be a man of vision fully equipped to set up the John Grooms Housing Association (JGHA), which came into being in 1970. In due course JGHA was able to qualify for Government grants under the Housing Act 1974 to meet the desperate shortage of wheelchair standard accommodation. He was a man of deep Christian faith, fully following the ethics of the nineteenth century's great Christian reformers, and perpetuating the same care and compassion. A very friendly man, he looked upon his staff as his most valuable asset and, like any good Captain of a ship, he kept his hands well on the helm of where Grooms was advancing.

Under his leadership, the housing programme just mushroomed. The first development had been Princess Crescent, mentioned in a previous chapter. The second development was in Holloway, North London, which opened early in 1977. Other wheelchair housing schemes in the London area, Bedfordshire, Bristol and Wiltshire were begun soon after. Since then, the expansion has been so vast, it is only possible in this short history to comment on a few.

Whitby Court in Holloway is part of a larger new estate and comprises a group of 12 ground floor flats specially designed for use by wheelchair tenants, which are managed within a larger complex of 64 units of general housing for which the Corporation of London are responsible. It differs from other sheltered schemes in that no alarms or emergency systems are installed and tenants are, despite serious disabilities, quite independent. Most of the folk who live here are in employment and travel to their jobs each day. Life for them is a little slower, a little harder, but there is no doubt about the success of the scheme.

Ross Court in Colindale, Middlesex, is another 'mixed' housing scheme having an emergency call system, including plans for an experimental flat-sharing scheme where able-bodied and disabled folk support each other.

Mardon House in Exeter was built in partnership with Exeter Health Authority and Exeter Community Health Trust and is now run by them. This residential unit provides long-term care and rehabilitation for up to twenty people. The centre incorporates some of the finest modern accessible design features; it also meets the needs of many other local wheelchair users, who have access to the superb re-ablement and physiotherapy facilities which exist at this project.

At Walsall in the West Midlands, John Grooms, in partnership with the Parkinson's Disease Society of the UK and Walsall Metropolitan Council, has built a revolutionary new housing scheme, the first of its kind in this country. It comprises nineteen one person flatlets, each with its own bathroom and kitchenette and each with easy access to central communal facilities. It provides a sheltered environment for people with Parkinson's Disease, so that they can live as independently as possible, while at the same time enjoying the care and security provided by a full-time warden and other support staff.

At Llantrisant in South Wales, is another housing development, the Maes Trisant flats. There are thirty-one of them and totally occupied by wheelchair users. Some flats have one bedroom, some two bedrooms and some three. There is an emergency call system, communal dining room/lounge, an assessment flat, medical room, guest room, assisted bath room, laundry and two lifts. The care staff are provided by Mid Glamorgan Social Services. They run a continuous shift for the seriously disabled tenants of which half a dozen are totally dependent at the time of writing. Vivian and Janet Price are scheme managers and on the day of my visit there I was warmed by their caring and obvious dedication. Vivian was tending the garden, while his wife, Janet, was cleaning up the hallway. Everywhere was spotless. Over a friendly cup of tea I found out a great deal more. Seriously disabled tenants are given an extensive trial and are only moved back into institutional life when it becomes a proven impossibility for them to manage. There was a cross section of disabilities in those resident at the time of my visit: spina bifida, multiple sclerosis, accidents and cerebral palsy. 'People may die – they don't just leave,' Janet answered cheerfully when I

Tenants at Brookdene Lodge, Swindon, relax in the courtyard

queried if they ever moved away, inferring, of course, that they were quite happy and content with their lives.

Brookdene Lodge at Haydon Wick, near Swindon, is another block of flats I have visited and been impressed by the efficiency and care with which the complex is run by the scheme managers Kjell and Gill Andersson. It provides 18 flats for physically disabled people and 17 units for mobile or able-bodied tenants. All the flats for physically disabled tenants are designed for wheelchair use, with wide doors and sympathetically planned kitchens and bathrooms. There is an emergency call system for the wheelchair units, and an important element in the scheme is the Common Room which can be used as a meeting place for the Residents' Association which has been formed. The building is also equipped with a small kitchen and a laundry room.

Testimonies continue to pour in showing the blessings and advantages of being able to live in one of the John Grooms Housing Association complexes, but space only permits quoting one or two from past and present.

Linda had been living in a residential home for seventeen years. She longed for greater independence and freedom. Then her mother heard about John Grooms Housing at an exhibition. When a vacancy arose, Linda moved in. She was delighted because she found the adaptions so unobtrusive. She hates sympathy and

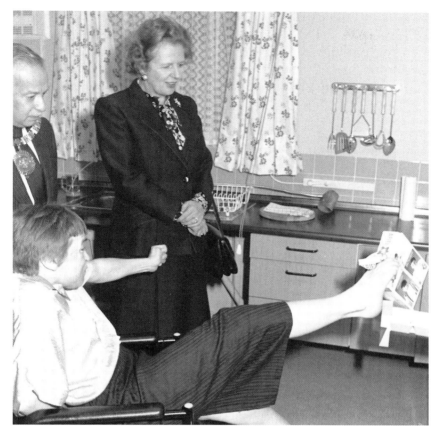

Sally demonstrating her low-level kitchen at Ash Close – to the then Prime Minister Margaret Thatcher

the flat gives her freedom to be herself. In the toilet she had to learn a new way of transferring, but otherwise there have been no major problems. She can get in and out of the bath alone, whereas before she had to rely on other people all the time.

Linda has a home help who cleans the floors and helps a little with shopping, but she enjoys housework and pottering around the flat. She also appreciates the opportunity to do her own cooking and entertaining, things that were difficult for her in the past. Now she finds it easy to have friends in for a chat or a drink. From her flat she can watch the children playing on an open green and she has a real sense of feeling part of the local community.

When Sally moved into a John Grooms flat it was the first time ever she had had a proper home of her own and she was delighted with it. Her disabilities were severe as she had hardly any control of her arms, but this encouraged her to become exceptionally adept at using her feet and toes. Toes and feet are used for putting soap powder into her washing machine. Her speech has been affected by her disability and she sometimes talks through a 'facilitator'. She has a beautiful poster adorning her lounge, which holds a message for us all. 'It is important to choose your own lifestyle and not let others choose it for you.' All these difficulties did not stop her from leading a full and rewarding life, even to working for a degree in contemporary studies.

Pamela is one of the liveliest people you could wish to meet. In her late forties, she is young at heart and bursting with mental energy and ideas – chiefly ideas on how to improve life for disabled people.

Pamela is herself severely disabled. She developed multiple sclerosis at the age of eighteen and moved with her parents to Canada from London in the hope that a change of climate would help her condition. The family left behind her brother, Reg, twenty years her senior. Pamela's English boyfriend followed her there, they married and Pamela worked as an executive secretary for six years. In 1970 she had a baby. 'After my daughter's birth, my health deteriorated and eventually I was confined to a wheelchair,' she says. Sadly, her marriage ended after twenty years and her brother agreed to look after her if she returned to England.

Pamela has become more determined and outspoken than ever as a result of her disability. She has collected an album which is brimming over with press cuttings, official letters and certificates resulting from her achievement as a spokesperson and lobbyist for disabled people in Canada. Now, in England, she hopes to continue her work, but the level of her disability is now so severe that living in an ordinary house would make life impossible.

Pamela is a tenant in a purpose-built, wheelchair standard two bedroom flat. She is cared for by her brother and a professional carer. 'We are so grateful to John Grooms for getting us here,' she says, looking with satisfaction around her tastefully decorated living room. 'Being here in this wheelchair-accessible flat has made all the difference.'

What more proof is needed to demonstrate that Grooms know exactly how to 'put themselves in another person's wheelchair?'

Chapter 12

LIVING OPTIONS

From 1984 onwards some very important events took place within the John Grooms development programme. That year Dolphin Court, built on the site of the former Thorpe Bay children's home, was opened by HRH The Duchess of Kent, who remarked that she had visited a large number of homes for disabled people, but this was the best she had seen.

A residential home, constructed at a cost of £850,000 and situated on the sea front at Thorpe Bay, it comprises flats for 15 disabled individuals and couples. As in all Grooms building complexes, each resident has his or her own kitchen, living room/bedroom and bathroom, with communal facilities available as well. One flat has been built for assessment purposes. This means that any disabled person can apply to spend a week or a fortnight in the flat so that they can determine whether, with the right aids and equipment, they could live independently if they wish to. Some stay longer while developing skills and confidence to take the next step to adapted housing in the community.

Derek and Jean Fletcher were the first managers of the complex and did a splendid job, not only coping with the physical disability problems of the residents, but showing insight into psychological difficulties. Some with severe disability could be highly motivated and need little encouragement to 'have a go!' Sometimes others with a lesser disability, not being of the same mould of character, needed more urging. Then there were times when physical disability was not the main problem at all. Those who were victims of the traumas and pressures of modern living needed a special kind of approach, which Mr and Mrs Fletcher tackled wisely despite feeling they did not have the specialised training for it.

Sarah, nineteen years old and affected by cerebral palsy, was

Dolphin Court – opening by HRH The Duchess of Kent, October 1984

their first resident. Having spent all her young life at boarding schools for disabled children, it was an entirely new experience for her. She was delighted at getting her specially adapted flat with her very own bathroom, kitchen and toilet, and making it her home. It takes Sarah longer to get dressed in the morning than an able-bodied person, but once in her wheelchair she is free to go out shopping and enjoy a much fuller life.

It is absolutely devastating to be told in your mid-twenties that you have multiple sclerosis. This is what happened to John. He was married at the time and tragically that marriage broke down. Several years later he met Jane at a multiple sclerosis centre and, despite the difficulties there were to overcome, they were able to marry. John could walk a little, but there came the time when he had to use a wheelchair. But they are happy and very grateful to John Grooms for providing them with accommodation.

Elizabeth and Terry were another couple who married despite severe disability. They were very happy, but sadly Elizabeth died quite suddenly only six months after their wedding, but not before being able to fulfil some of their longings and ambitions. Shortly before she died, Elizabeth wrote an article on Dolphin Court expressing her appreciation. It was entitled, 'Heaven on Earth.' Here is part of what she said:

Welcome to Dolphin Court, Thorpe Bay

'Here in the care of the most wonderful Christian staff who are so kind, nothing is too much trouble for them. We have a lovely view from our flat with a balcony with a bird table and a space to grow flowers.'

Another couple, Hugh and Carol, married for eleven years, and both seriously disabled by cerebral palsy, cope very well as long as someone is near at hand to help at the right moment – a help Dolphin Court supplies. Hugh has no control of his upper limbs, but performs marvels with his feet, operating a computer for a local film company. He has also designed his own eating aid to use in the privacy of his flat. He testifies that Dolphin Court satisfied their needs emotionally and physically.

Martin, a sufferer from Friedreich's Ataxia, was cared for by his mother in an upstairs flat until he could no longer walk. Becoming wheelchair bound left him trapped in his own environment. He explains 'I couldn't walk downstairs; two chaps on the Queensway staff (a Community Activity Centre) very kindly said "OK, we'll come along and carry you downstairs." I put up with it for a while, but in the end it was beginning to affect my dignity, because I felt I was being treated like a sack of potatoes. So I thought "John Grooms, please accept me," and they did!'

When I recently visited Dolphin Court some had moved on, but Martin was still there. It was a sparkling sunny day and my first impression was how 'new' the building appeared. Facing the sea I had thought it would be looking slightly 'weather-worn' after eleven years. And this 'shining' impression remained with me as Richard Hale, the Regional Manager, took me through a pretty little garden and into the dining room for lunch. A main meal is served five times during the week. Other meals are prepared in the residents' flats by themselves, though help is always given where needed. Martin was there enjoying a meal with his friends and afterwards gave me a conducted tour of his flat. He told me that when he had first considered going to Dolphin Court, he had thought he would be going into a community of some kind and certainly not into the life he had found it to be. He still enjoyed going to the Queensway to meet with his friends, and his mother visits him too.

As I looked round the flat he had so obviously made his home with wall posters, music centre and shelves crammed with knick-knacks, tapes and books and its balcony beyond overlooking the sparkling sea, I felt there was no need to ask the question that I did: 'Are you happy here?' 'Over the moon,' he answered, and that said it all!

In 1992, nominated by Martin and another resident of Dolphin Court, Mandy Herman, Grooms again won a major award as Dolphin Court was named 'Care Home of the Year' by a panel of judges headed by Lady Wagner, who also led the Government appointed Commission investigating standards in residential care. Richard Hale was Manager at that time – the Fletchers had moved on to a new and similar complex at Norwich by then – and he and his team beat fifty-six other contenders to claim this accolade, the 'caring' equivalent of the FA cup!

To celebrate and commemorate the occasion, Martin and Mandy composed the following poem:

> *We see them come, we see them go,*
> *Where they end up we like to know,*
> *Maybe to the left or to the right,*
> *Dolphin Court helps make life bright!*
> *Encouraged by staff, we learn the skills*
> *to fight off foes and obstacles,*
> *Our life is eased by caring people*
> *With whom we live from day to day,*
> *And who show us how to make our way.*
>
> *On winter days the flats are warm,*
> *With heaters on and curtains drawn,*
> *We settle down away from harm,*
> *To watch TV or tell a yarn,*
> *In summertime, when it is hot,*
> *We're glad we're in a seaside spot,*
> *To watch the boats and people walk,*
> *On the beach and along the wall.*
>
> *Our drop-in day, to Richard's glee,*
> *Was full of fun and frivolity,*
> *Abseiling down the outside wall,*
> *To entertain the watching crowd,*
> *We reached the ground, wheelchairs'n'all.*
>
> *The likes of us who need a 'fort'*
> *Are pleased to be in Dolphin Court,*
> *Where training is good, and restrictions nought.*
> *Friendly carers with their support*
> *Make things happen to us all,*
> *To leave this place is our aim,*
> *With extra skills that we can gain,*
> *To join the rest of you out there,*
> *With confidence, and things to share.*

The abseiling mentioned in the poem was launched by the residents and staff themselves as a fund raiser. A group of abseilers

'She'll be coming down the mountain' – Michelle shows her daring by abseiling down Dolphin Court back wall

fixed their gear to the roof, including the gear for wheelchair abseiling. Sponsors were invited and the Southend Friends joined in. Several of the residents responded just for the fun of it.

The Southend Friends of John Grooms perform an excellent job of fund raising, with the guidance of Miss Denise Smith. Denise was their Chairman for a long time but has recently become Vice Chairman and Beverley Ford has now taken the Chair. Once they held a 'Dog Jog'. Dogs of all shapes and sizes turned up on the day, all excited at the thought of 'walkies' around a car park. Chris Serle (of 'That's Life' fame) agreed to come along to start the joggers and help collect money from the sightseers. Unfortunately he got lost in the back streets of Southend and was late arriving, but he soon made up lost time by signing autographs and kissing several ladies and babies in return for a donation in his collecting box – by the end of the day it was very heavy! And all the dogs behaved perfectly!

Money has also been raised by carol singing, having a runner in the London Marathon, and concerts compered by Richard

Martin with Mayor of Southend at the Southend Friends' stall on August Bank Holiday 1994

Baker, Roger Royle and Chris Serle – the music being provided by local choirs and school orchestras. Their plans are so versatile and numerous – even to the extent of kidnapping an MP (a willing victim!) and holding him to ransom! It is impossible to list them all. The Southend Friends raised the funds to purchase the very useful and well used ambulance bus at Dolphin Court and they also fundraise to serve the needs of three other Grooms complexes in the Southend area, Beresford Close, Southbourne Grove and Stambridge Road. Grooms also receive active support for their work from Jennie and Alfred Groom, descendants of the Founder, who live in the Southend locality. They have hosted many events over the years in their house and garden – Bring and Buy sales, coffee mornings, garden parties etc. and have for many years sold quantities of Christmas cards.

The three homes mentioned above opened in 1989 and 1990 after several years of deliberation by the then Southend Health Authority, as to the future of patients living in Carisbrooke Ward, the Young Disabled Unit, and the needs of people requiring long term care in the community and in hospital. The general philosophy was then formulated and the search began to find suitable houses to adapt to rehouse people from the Ward in as pleasant an environment as possible. John Grooms then became involved as the managing body and has been responsible for the day to day management and ongoing development of the service ever since. As these homes offer long term accommodation for people with severe physical disabilities, vacancies do not occur very often.

I visited Beresford Close on the same day that I visited Dolphin Court and my first impression upon seeing it was, 'What a dear little place,' and I felt just as happy about it when I went inside. A low ceilinged bungalow type of building, it had a cosy aspect, added to by the paintings lying around in the living room and the half finished one left propped on the easel by a gentleman severely handicapped by multiple sclerosis who they were caring for. He had been admitted to hospital for skin grafts and wound cleansing, and then, because the hospital needed the bed, he had been sent on to Beresford Close for the healing of pressure sores and the correction of malnutrition. He lives as active a life as possible and loves painting. Beresford only has room for five or six people and those I met in the lounge were as friendly and chatty as any small family. You would never have recognised it as a nursing home. To me it was just 'home' – and the credit in no small measure, I am sure, must go to Pat Cluness, the very friendly day manager who obviously loved her charges and was planning to take them all out to dinner that evening to celebrate someone's birthday.

Stambridge Road might be referred to as 'country cousin' to the other two homes. It too is a bungalow, a registered Residential Care Home with Rochford town centre only half a mile away, but still only a short walk from open farmland. However, it is a larger bungalow set back from the road behind other houses and, designed with wheelchair users in mind, it has wide corridors and easy access to all rooms. But there are still only six permanent residents cared for here, accommodated in four single and one shared room. All bedrooms are pleasantly furnished with washbasins, Hi-low beds, double wardrobes, drawer units and bedside tables, T/V, phone socket and call system. The large lounge and dining area has a brick built fireplace with a wood burning stove, the envy of all the other homes. This is lit to impress visitors in the winter, but causes staff and residents to expire with the heat! The lounge overlooks a large patio and garden. There is a large kitchen with a low work surface for residents wishing to use it. A large bathroom with a Parker bath and a shower room plus toilets, are all on the main corridor, as is the laundry and linen room. Staff feel they cannot leave out reference to Carrie, the cat, whom they describe as 'warm and friendly'. All staff receive appropriate training to care for and support residents who for a variety of reasons have chosen to come into residential accommodation. The staffing levels are consistent with other homes in Southend, three staff in the

Residents relaxing at Stambridge Road, Rochford, Essex

morning and never less than two at any other time, including nights. The manager is a registered nurse but, as in any other care home, the District Nurses are available to clients who are assessed as requiring this service.

Southbourne Grove is a quite different building. It is a large detached 1930's style house in a residential area of Westcliff-on-Sea and it has been adapted to provide accommodation on two levels with an easily managed lift available to residents. It is run on exactly the same lines as the other two and furnished very similarly, with rooms for five permanent residents plus one short stay respite care. Like the other homes it has a shared gardener/driver/handyperson, plus shared clerical assistant/activities organiser. Last, but by no means least, this house, too, has a cat, only he is of the opposite gender – and called Charlie! It also has a very pleasant patio and a lovely large garden. Staff training relevant to the needs of people with physical disabilities is important to John Grooms as an organisation. Training for National Vocational Qualifications (NVQ's) for some staff takes place in all three Southend homes, as in others.

About a mile from the centre of Norwich is another important development of Grooms – John Grooms Court which was completed in May 1989. As with Dolphin Court, the Association's then Chairman, His Honour Judge Alan Hitching, was delighted to welcome HRH The Duchess of Kent, our Patron, to officially 'open' the new building. The Duchess toured the project, chatted to the young people who would be using the 22 flat complex as a starting point for a life of their own, and was impressed with the standard of facilities and the new ideas being put into practice. With the experience gained from running Dolphin Court, Derek and Jean Fletcher moved in as managers and, Grooms being in the forefront all the way along in caring for disabled people, it is their opinion that John Grooms Court is even a further step ahead in training young disabled people to go out and live within the community. The local Social Services personnel were amazed at the disabled people who did manage, not imagining some of them could ever live independently.

Linda, for instance, is a real success story. After living at John Grooms Court for four years learning to cope with, and to master, the everyday tasks and chores that present real problems to the severely handicapped, she learnt to cope so well that she felt able to leave and start her life anew in a home that she could truly call her own. She says 'I never dreamed that I would be moving into my own place, but here I am living in my very own specially-adapted bungalow. Of course it hasn't been easy, but with the help of the John Grooms staff, I've learnt how to cope on my own.'

And there are many others like Linda. Her story is not unique. Rather, it is typical. As the numbers of disabled people in our society grow, and as the resources made available to them from central and local government are more thinly spread, so organisations such as Grooms, which was founded well before the welfare state ever existed, will play an ever more important role in the lives of so many disabled people.

In the UK today one person in ten is disabled. One in four families has a disabled member. Many people are seeking accessible accommodation and this social need will rise inexorably with the years. It will be a problem that will not go away.

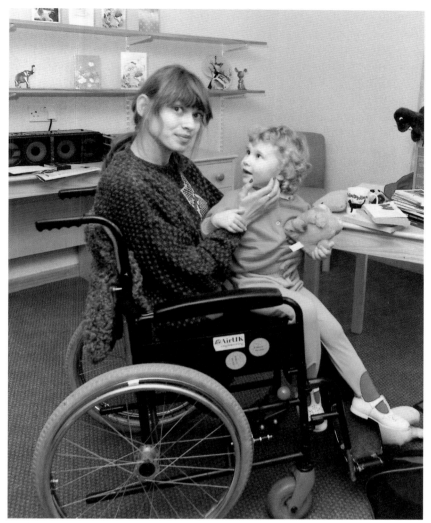

Linda at John Grooms Court, Norwich

As with Dolphin Court, there are 'Friends of John Grooms Court' too, who are active and supportive. In seven years the Friends raised over £63,000 which was largely spent in purchasing a mini-bus and, amongst other things, a spare electric wheelchair, a one-wheelchair vehicle, Baby Belling cookers, a carpet cleaner and a fax machine. They have shared in the growth and development of the Court from its beginning and, as Derek Fletcher remarked in an interview for the Newsletter: 'It is difficult to actually put into words what help we require from our

Friends. Whatever we ask of their Chairman, Wendy Moulton, the Friends always rise to the occasion.'

Mr and Mrs Fletcher have now gone into well earned retirement but, in a recent interview, Jean mentioned a lovely little happening at Dolphin Court. In Jean's own words: 'A lady just came in off the street one day and asked if it was John Grooms and could she have a look round. One of the care staff then took her around and although she didn't say anything to us, she wrote in the Visitor's Book: "My great grandfather, John Groom, would be very proud of this." She came from Canada – didn't say anything to us, just drifted in and drifted out. It was so sad. I don't know whether she ever came back after that, but it was a lovely surprise when we looked in the book after she had gone.'

As touched on earlier in this history, with so many accidents taking place, and the tensions and stresses of modern living, the Fletchers were sometimes finding borderline problems creeping in. These could tend to be a greater handicap to overcome than the physical disability and they felt that specialised training was

The Icanho project (proposed brain injury unit), Stowmarket – an artist's impression

required. So Grooms have taken another step forward by forming a partnership with Suffolk Health Authority and Suffolk Social Services to establish a new community-based Rehabilitation Centre for people who have suffered brain injury. Recent reports produced by the Royal College of Physicians and the Royal Hospital and Home, Putney have highlighted the inadequate provision for the long-term requirements of people with a brain injury. In Suffolk, the Regional Health Authority has drawn attention to the immediate and urgent need in allocating resources to give people with brain damage a real priority – in order that the development of avoidable behavioural and emotional problems can be prevented. In 1993 nearly 500 adults in Suffolk alone sustained a brain injury through accident, strokes or disease. The effects can be devastating both for the people affected and their families. The first six months are crucial to successful recovery but at present there is no specialised, co-ordinated help offering a full range of rehabilitative services in that county. Grooms have therefore been approached by the Health Authority and County Council to design an innovative Brain Injuries Rehabilitation Unit that will address the whole range of clinical and therapeutic needs resulting from a brain injury. It is planned to become nationally known as a centre of excellence providing a 'seamless' service. Taking over when intensive hospital care stops, its major aim will be to help patients' integration into the community.

Grooms also manages another care home within the Suffolk and Essex boundaries – this is 'Treetops' at Colchester. The property is owned by the local Health Authority and it is a Nursing/Residential Home for young, physically disabled people, situated on the Highwoods Estate on the northern edge of Colchester. There are sixteen spacious single rooms all with en-suite shower room and kitchen facilities. The aim of the staff is to provide a living environment in which residents can feel comfortable and secure, to provide stimulation and encouragement for each person, to assist them to reach their potential and fulfil their physical, emotional and spiritual needs.

Within a few months of the opening of 'Treetops', Sheila Bassilious, the Manager of the unit, soon realised, from her own observations and the enquiries being received, that there was a large number of disabled people living in the Colchester area who lived in their own homes but needed help to cope with the personal care needs. With the implementation of 'Care in the Community' in April 1993 it would then be possible for Social

Colchester Community Care Service launch at 'Treetops' (April 1993)

Services care managers to 'buy in' tailored care packages for those people rather than rely on the very limited and unstructured help previously available from the home help and district nursing services. Although there were, of course, existing agencies handling the care needs of predominantly elderly people, there was a dearth of provision for young physically disabled people. This prompted Sheila to suggest to David Newnham, Grooms Director of Services & Development, that there was a 'niche market' there waiting to be tapped and 'shouldn't Grooms do something about it?' The Care Committee of Grooms quickly agreed to the set-up of a pilot Community Care Service in December 1992 which would be run initially from 'Treetops' but use 'outside' care staff employed part-time on an agency basis. This service was an immediate success and grew substantially so that by 1995 it was essential to move the Community Care

Service office out of 'Treetops' into premises nearby rented from Tesco. Soon a similar service was to be started based on the Jane Hodge Hotel in South Wales.

Yet another project Grooms is more than pleased to control is HOPE Nursery, situated in Barrow Lane, Cheshunt, within the area of the Lea Valley – HOPE being an acronym for 'Horticultural Opportunities for Purposeful Employment'. The nursery was officially opened on 18th April 1984 by the well-known broadcaster of 'Gardeners' Question Time', Professor Alan Gemmell of Keele University, but HOPE had been in operation in fact, for almost a year before that. The vision for the project came originally from the staff at the Occupational Therapy department at Chase Farm Hospital, Enfield. They had started a small horticultural therapy section at the hospital psychiatric unit several years earlier, but had come to realise that there was a need of a 'half-way house' between hospital and open employment. A scheme based on a commercial horticultural holding was enthusiastically received at a public meeting convened at the hospital in 1981 and John Grooms Association for Disabled People, who were represented at that meeting, were asked to take the proposition under their wing and to turn the idea into reality.

The Committee made a full investigation, including commissioning a feasibility study by consultants 'Horticultural Therapy'. Horticultural units run by several other disabled persons' organisations, including one by Remploy at Wisbech, were visited. Then, with 75% capital grant–aid and part revenue deficit funding offered from the Manpower Services Commission (now called 'The Employment Service'), Grooms agreed to back the project and provide the balance of the capital funds, using its fundraising department's expertise. It proved a lengthy search before a suitable site could be found, but at the right moment in time, the miracle happened. A 2.9 acre holding was discovered in Barrow Lane, Cheshunt, Hertfordshire, and after negotiation, was purchased freehold for only £32,000. What is more, it had the advantage of existing glasshouses and local public transport, although two of the eight glasshouses had to be completely rebuilt and reglazed. An additional quarter acre Venlo type glasshouse was subsequently constructed on the site together with a mess room and packing/storage building with good wheelchair access. More recently, the whole of the original 30-year-old wooden-framed glasshouses were demolished to make way for modern high efficiency aluminium-framed greenhouses.

Pauline demonstrates plant propagation to disabled staff at HOPE Nursery

Disabled staff tidy up hanging baskets at HOPE, ready for market

Manager Michael Clarke with staff at HOPE Nursery giving the geraniums a routine quality check

John Grooms HOPE Nursery stand at Chelsea Flower Show, with workers Bernie and Lee

The crops selected for production had to be ones which require manual work. There was no point in attempting to grow crops which others commercially harvest mechanically, as the result is quite uneconomic. Therefore propagation work was more practical and satisfying – workers could see the results of their work day by day. The ability and preferences of workers have to be taken into account – some are dextrous and cope well with propagation or seed sowing; others are more suited to the heavier manual work such as concreting paths, digging, repairing fences and general maintenance on the Nursery site. Generally the atmosphere is a happy one, but there can be difficulties. Work pressure can prove a problem for many disabled people, especially those with an emotional or mental handicap, and repeated time off sick when the pressure mounts is indicative that personal limits of coping are being reached. Nonetheless, some enjoy the challenge of pressure and it is notable that the younger workers really appreciate the chance to work; they do not like the attitude that the 'world owes them a living.' Calm ones help the newcomers and even the simplest tasks achieved are a real encouragement to those initially lacking confidence in themselves.

One of the first disabled workers employed at HOPE commented:

> 'I'd been out of work over two years when the hospital (Chase Farm) told me about John Grooms plan to open HOPE Nursery and I applied straight away. I am very pleased to work here doing a job I like. It has changed my life and given me real hope for the future.'

When I spoke to the Nursery manager during my recent visit, he told me the personal stories of two former employees at HOPE and the way they had been helped:

> 'Chris is blind, and he came to work at HOPE because he wanted to learn more about commercial horticulture. He has a guide-dog called Gary, who leads him everywhere, and we were amazed that he could find his way to the Nursery from Cuffley Station each day. He has his own special way of potting-up and planting, and can do most tasks. He left us in order to go to Lincoln Agricultural (Horticultural) College, and is now running his own business growing and selling geraniums, fuchsias and bedding plants from his own greenhouses.'
> 'Gary (another former employee – not Chris's guide dog!)

used to work for us six years ago. He came to us not having done anything much that was in any way useful. His parents quickly told us it was a waste of time him coming here because he couldn't do anything. Anyway, we gave him a trial week and it was quite clear that he was not useless, but was highly trainable. Within about three months he was showing other people how to do things. His main "disability" appeared to be dyslexia, apart from being a slow learner. He went on and took a course in horticulture at Capel Manor, and a special oral examination was produced for him, as he could neither read nor write. He now works for Capel Manor as a full-time groundsman.'

And to highlight some of the mental and personality problems involved, the manager quotes the following:

'One young man has an impediment in speaking, and also learning difficulties. Ask him to add up three five figure numbers and he will do it in his head, but he is very slow at understanding practical tasks. He is quite small and most of our other workers tower over his head. One day a rather large employee decided to pick a fight with him and frightened him severely. The result was that two weeks later all his hair was falling out and before long he was completely bald, arms, eye-brows, eye-lashes – everything. His hair did grow again but, three years later, the same person picked a fight with him again. Once more all his hair fell out, and he became suicidal. It took a long time for him to come to terms with having no hair and Pauline, my wife, had to try to convince him that lots of other lads were shaving their heads in order to be in the fashion! But he has now settled down well and the trouble maker has been sacked. The hair is beginning to come back in clumps and he is a very happy worker.'

Michael Clarke was managing the complex when I visited it on a pleasant spring day, and the sheer size of it left me gasping. A vast vista of seedlings met the eye, as though some giant invisible hand had brought them all to the same height at the same time! The more advanced plants at that moment ran to 8,000 hydrangeas, 17,000 big geraniums, 150,000 smaller ones and 150,000 fuchsias – and that was just for starters – it was impossible to take in all the panorama. Michael had had a broad experience in the Nursery industry and had thoroughly enjoyed his job, though he has since moved on and the nursery is now under new management.

Over one million top quality house plants are grown at

HOPE each year – supplying some of the best known stores throughout Britain. Some fifty different species are reared from seed and cuttings, including many overseas varieties. And apart from major regular contracts with supermarkets, HOPE sells regularly to local shops, garden centres, other growers and secondary wholesalers (who sell on to retail shops). Competition is a constant factor, not only from other growers in the UK, Holland and Denmark, but now from Israel, Sri Lanka, Korea and Taiwan as well. HOPE also exports some of its knowledge and enquiries have been received from India and South Africa from people who hope to set up similar horticultural training establishments for disabled people in their own countries.

Foliage plants are a specialisation which Michael Clarke introduced to HOPE Nursery when he joined Grooms in 1985 and in which he is highly skilled. This range of crops produces a good return and now accounts for almost half of the total production. Hydrangeas, geraniums, fuchsias, poinsettias and bedding plants are all firm favourites and enjoy heavy sales for high quality markets. The detailed cropping programme is phased on a monthly basis throughout the year to maximise the use of the available glasshouse space, although the programme is necessarily adjusted from time to time depending on the skills and experience gained by the disabled horticultural workers, market conditions and commercial considerations generally. There is keen awareness of the need for steadily developing and widening its clientele – dependence upon too few customers is potentially dangerous.

Newcomers usually come for an introductory few days' trial; slow learners are usually accompanied by their Social worker. They are introduced to two or three other workers so that they can get to know someone, and then they work alongside one person for a couple of days to get to 'know the ropes.' Simple tasks like putting pots on trays are given at this stage. Plants are grown in 'plugs' these days which makes it easier with less risk of damage to the plant by unskilled or clumsy handling. The objective of this initial period is to make the new disabled worker feel they are doing a real job of work so that they are encouraged to hold their heads high and feel proud of the Nursery and the part they are playing.

The development of groups of three or four workers, with a team leader, is proving an effective way of organising the work in the Nursery. It enables a 'revolving' pattern of work to be offered. Some disabled workers, however, are averse to any change as it leads to a feeling of insecurity. National Vocational Qualifications (NVQs) are now being offered through the 'Investors in People' programme recently started. Individual personal plans are being developed for each worker over the coming year or two and a prototype plan has already been successfully piloted. This will enable the work of each individual to be properly logged and progressed.

Geoffrey Hamilton, presenter of BBC TV's 'Gardener's World', is among the many visitors to HOPE each year. When he first visited the Nursery to open a new cold greenhouse, he was very impressed. 'I had imagined a sheltered workshop with a few plants.... what I found was a professional "state of the art" nursery, with a competent and capable workforce competing on an equal footing in the market place.' Marion Rowe (formerly the local MP and now an MEP) has also visited, and Mrs Norma Major came on a private tour of the Nursery in November 1994, after being impressed by her visits on two separate occasions to the Grooms stand at the Chelsea flower show. Other well known personalities have visited over the years, and all have been impressed by the standard of work and products being sold. It must be stressed that plants are readily sold on their sheer commercial high quality, and not the fact that disabled people grow them.

And it crosses my mind to ponder what John Groom, the Founder, would think could he, too, like other important personages cross that Nursery threshold today. Would he consider what a long way from those watercress days Grooms had travelled? Would he be utterly amazed that somewhere along the line the artificial flowers had become real ones?

But can we not be sure of one thing? – his gratification summed up for HOPE in the young man's words: 'I am very pleased to work here doing a job I like. It has changed my life and given me real hope for the future.'

Chapter 13

INDEPENDENT HOUSING

By 1987 the pattern of building blocks of flats – or developments incorporating housing units for wheelchair users with able-bodied people – had changed. These were proving large and expensive and, as a result, limiting the amount of development in any given area. The desire of disabled people is to live within the community where the next door neighbour is not a wheelchair user and they can live as independently as possible. Therefore the Association embarked upon a programme of partnerships with other Housing Associations and developers who were producing general needs and family housing. The resultant product was to integrate wheelchair units within new developments. A great deal of negotiation with other organisations has been necessary and the Association is now working in partnership with more than 40 others.

One such scheme is the St John's project next to what was, until recently, Grooms head office in Finsbury Park. It provides a range of wheelchair friendly houses, bungalows and flats as well as general needs housing, totalling 40 units. This scheme Grooms have built in partnership with the Apna Ghar Housing Association, who specialise in wheelchair housing for disabled people from Asian backgrounds and who will manage nine of the units. The Association has also built a new church and vicarage for the Diocese of London, replacing St John's Church, which had become structurally unsafe and originally occupied the site.

Housing schemes with managers continued to answer the need for a certain group of disabled people. The Association has been particularly blessed with a goodly number of men and women who have felt the call to become scheme managers and who serve their tenants well; they are a group of people who go the extra mile and conform in every way to the ethos of the

The St John's, Hackney, development at Finsbury Park nearing completion, including a new church

HRH The Prince of Wales meets tenants at Wylye Lodge, Wilton, following opening

Association. An outstanding example was Mr. Norman Loasby, who, after retiring following nine years' service as Housing Manager, went on to manage the new development at Wilton, near Salisbury, where he welcomed HRH The Prince of Wales to officially open the scheme in November 1987. Here Norman

JGHA stand at the annual exhibition and conference of Institute of Housing, Harrogate (1994)

served warm-heartedly and faithfully until his life's end, another eight years later.

Following the geographical spread of the Association's building programme from the existing areas of North London, down the M4 corridor into the South and the West to Swindon, Salisbury, Bristol and South Wales, its operations then spread North-East into Essex and northwards towards the Midlands. Places like Milton Keynes and Birmingham became growth areas for development. In both instances, the Local Authority knew what its need was for disabled people's housing and was prepared to back a specialist Housing Association like John Grooms to achieve its objective in providing a balanced housing programme.

The results of a research project carried out by the Housing Corporation, supported by John Grooms and published in 1991, revealed the astonishing fact that a further 330,000 wheelchair housing units were needed in Great Britain, and this did not include those 36,000 young people currently living in residential homes.

The aim of John Grooms Housing Association (JGHA) is to meet this challenge. Our inception in 1969 looked forward to the day when expertise such as ours would be called upon by local authorities and other developers and housing associations to join with them to **build for the future**. It was this aim that led JGHA

Sir George Young, Bt MP, Minister for Housing & Planning, opens Peel Close, Chingford

to exhibit regularly at the Chartered Institute of Housing annual exhibition and conference at Harrogate to increase awareness of what John Grooms could offer.

In the autumn of 1995 I was privileged to be conducted on a tour of Peel Close, Chingford. This project had been constructed and opened by Grooms three years earlier in partnership with the Circle 33 Housing Trust; it was Grooms first development of two-storey **houses** fully designed to wheelchair standards. The scheme received considerable acclaim and when Sir George Young, the then Housing Minister, came to see it he was most impressed.

The housing estate lay in a cul-de-sac off the main thoroughfare and my first impression was that they were houses of character. The six Grooms ones nestling amongst them were no different at all in outer appearance, each having an attractive front and back garden with the main door at the side of the house approached by a wide driveway.

I was meant to visit Nigel and his brood of lively children, but unfortunately it was one of his bad times. Nigel has multiple sclerosis. Prior to coming to Peel Close his worries were added to in that he and his wife and two young children were living in a one bedroom flat. Not only could he no longer manage stairs, but the flat was too small, and it was therefore difficult for him to use his wheelchair. He was reduced to crawling around the flat until the opportunity came for him to live in this John Grooms house. 'Had we been able to afford it ourselves, we couldn't have bought a better house,' he commented on moving in. Now he is fully mobile, able to get to every part of the house on both floors, has added to his family with a further child, and cannot believe his good fortune.

Since Nigel's house was not available for inspection, we visited wheelchair user Barbara instead, who, with her able-bodied husband, had moved to this 'lovely house' as she referred to it, which could not be faulted in any direction. Constructed to Grooms usual fully designed wheelchair standard, it boasted an 'extra'. A vertical lift had been included, neatly tucked away behind the staircase, but it was a lift with a difference. I was intrigued by the device beneath it which brought it to an automatic halt if anyone or anything intruded beneath it – a vital safety measure if children should be romping over every part of the house. The bathroom designed to wheelchair standards upstairs also enabled disabled parents to participate in their children's bath time. No wonder Sir George Young had commented of the development: 'I think this does show what can be done with initiative and enthusiasm. We need more of this.'

JGHA continues the link which its sister charity (John Grooms Association for Disabled People) has had with the Corporation of London since its foundation. When London's Lady Mayoress made her annual visit to Grooms Edgware Estate at the commencement of one of JGHA's projects, she was invited to lay the foundation stone of 'Roseway' – a new purpose designed block of flats replacing the house of the same name that had been erected on the same site over sixty years earlier. In due course the charity's President, the Archbishop of Canterbury, Dr. George Carey, came to perform the opening ceremonies of these flats and another scheme named 'Brookside' at Edgware. During this time, he visited a number of new tenants and spent some time talking with them. Together with his wife, he stayed for the afternoon and concluded his visit with a discussion with Committee members and senior staff to understand more of the

Rosemary in the kitchen of her wheelchair flat at Roseway

complexities of producing disabled people's housing and care. Grooms are indeed blessed with a President who shows an interest in the work and attends whenever possible.

One of the greatest highlights in the life of the Housing Association was the Service of Thanksgiving held in Westminster Abbey in November 1992 in celebration of 21 years of JGHA's existence. The Abbey was packed with supporters and friends. People involved in different aspects of the Association's work took part in the service and the final address was given by the Rev. Clive Calver, Director General of the Evangelical Alliance.

An important aspect is the involvement of JGHA in the National Wheelchair Housing Association Group (NATWHAG). This is an organisation first started from an idea by John Grooms which enables other housing associations, also involved in

Outside Westminster Abbey before the 21st anniversary service

wheelchair housing, to gather together and present a united front to Government and other statutory authorities. The influence of the Group has been considerable and has helped bring the needs of disabled people to the attention of people of influence in the housing world. Regular meetings with the Chairman and senior executives of the Housing Corporation and the Minister for Housing have taken place.

JGHA sought to build upon the many contacts that it was making. A particular partnership was made with the Guinness Trust, a well respected foundation providing social housing for families. Already several schemes have been completed with them and others are in the pipeline.

Another area of activity which JGHA was approached to assist in was that of head injury. The Icanho project in Suffolk is already under way by the charity and has been outlined in another chapter, but several other schemes have been developed by JGHA. The first was at Stoke Mandeville in Buckinghamshire. It provides a much needed facility which is appreciated so much by the relatives who have not known which way to turn when suddenly confronted by a new and disastrous situation. Someone near to them has become brain damaged and they wish to provide for their new limited capacity in the best way possible. With 300 in every 100,000 people suffering a severe brain injury, John Grooms is committed to this group of people for whom independent living has for too long seemed out of reach. JGHA has appointed the Disabled Housing Trust, who are specialists in this field, to manage the scheme and provide the care. Grooms were particularly privileged that Her Royal Highness the Duchess of Kent came to open the scheme – a scheme that benefits people like Kevin, who sustained a head injury following a road accident 17 years ago, when he was living with his parents. He comments: 'I am so happy getting a place of my own – my Mum and Dad will not be in charge of me any more. It will give them a break. I am looking forward to living in my own flat.'

With the change in some disabled people's financial position, often brought about through receiving compensation as the result of an accident, they can find themselves with the means of at least part purchasing a property, and the Association has therefore looked into opportunities for shared ownership projects. Another area of need has been for people who have multiple disabilities. In many instances, these are people who are currently living within a long stay psychiatric hospital which is destined for closure. Their needs require careful assessment, yet this group of people are often the last to be resettled or re-accommodated. Even though their disability is considerable, with the right kind of accommodation and proper care, their future can be enhanced and made more enjoyable. John Grooms is in contact with a number of Hospital Trusts planning for these schemes.

Janice is severely disabled. She had been in an institution since childhood and, after attending a training centre, wanted to live within the community. By becoming one of Grooms tenants, though still receiving all the considerable care she needed, she achieved her aim. She was able to communicate her wishes via her computer and, by the same process, showed a lot of initiative by writing her life story. One of her greatest hopes had been to raise a family and, following her marriage, she subsequently had her first child. The only difficulty was that John Grooms did not, at that time, have a large enough housing unit in the area for her family. Janice moved back to Ireland, but in due course applied to John Grooms to return when suitably sized accommodation became available.

In the midst of these developments, JGHA has been faced with many changes. The funding arrangements involving housing have altered on several occasions. The most major change was in 1989, since when the amount of grant being made available by the Government has been substantially reduced, resulting in the need to obtain considerable funds on mortgage loans from banks, building societies and the private financial market.

With expansion and the increasing complexities of the development programme, staffing of all JGHA's departments has had to be built up and, where necessary, restructured to ensure that properly qualified and experienced people are responsible for managing the day-to-day activities of the Association. Grooms are fortunate in having dedicated staff thoroughly committed in their care for disabled people. Many late nights have been spent debating the finer points of the organisation's future, of how to provide as many housing units as possible at a reasonable cost, but still maintaining a high standard. Regular conferences are held where policy issues can be debated and training provided. Disabled people feature increasingly on the Association's Committees and are fast becoming decision makers. The organisation is becoming more consumer-led, with notice being taken of tenants' comments via surveys and questionnaires. A large amount of information is collected from tenants and fed back to our development team.

John Grooms Housing Association is able to be part of a unique partnership because of its relationship with John Grooms Association for Disabled People. Although separately staffed and separately governed, the two organisations are in the same building and, wherever possible, work together and mutually benefit each other. The result is that officers of both organisations are able to offer to statutory bodies a deal which includes the most essential aspects of independence for disabled people. This ranges from residential care to training centres for independent living within the community and, where necessary – sadly sometimes the case – a return to residential care. John Grooms can offer a range of opportunities which are not available elsewhere. JGHA has now grown to be the leading provider of wheelchair housing in England. To be able to offer this, along with the provision of care, is the answer to many people's problems and requests. For this reason it has been necessary for the two organisations to build up a network of mutual involvement, for staff to communicate closely with each other and their committees meet for joint conferences. John Grooms is committed to doing its best to influence

JGHA's Committee of Management in session at Finsbury Park

Government departments to make proper provision for this large group of people, who are beginning to voice their own needs, and are looking to organisations like Grooms to provide the means.

The complete list of John Grooms Housing Association developments to date (see Appendix B) surely demonstrates not only why they are the leading provider of wheelchair housing in England, but reveals how much they care. Without this driving incentive, it could not be so. This care and concern our donors show they share with us, for without their ongoing generosity this great work could not continue. No one needs telling that housing is costly and, as already mentioned, Government grants have been considerably reduced. Public support is all the more urgently needed to provide the additional features that enable even severely disabled people to achieve the greatest possible level of **independence**.

Chapter 14

A RATHER SPECIAL SERVICE

St. George's Day 1991 will live long in the memory of 2,500 people: not only because of the celebration of England's patron saint, but because they were privileged to be present in St. Paul's Cathedral at a Service of Thanksgiving to mark the 125th Anniversary of the founding of John Grooms Association for Disabled People.

Planning had been going on for months beforehand, meetings held with the St. Paul's clergy, representatives of the London Fire Brigade and the City of London Police. Problems of all kinds had to be solved. Invitation lists had to be drawn up, printing designs agreed upon, transport and parking arranged, hymns chosen and people invited to take part in the Service.

Barbara Edwards, who was secretary to the director, and her husband Ted and their helpers, sent out the invitations, but a lot more people wanted to come than St. Paul's could possibly accommodate.

I was one of the fortunate ones to be invited, but on the morning of 23rd April, being driven by car, I chafed at our slow progress through the streets of the busy Capital. Mixed in with my thoughts, too, was my curiosity as to just how Grooms were going to solve the problem of all those steps, only to discover on my arrival at the last minute that St. Paul's had been given three enormous ramps – one at the Great West Door and the other two round at the North side. When Sir Christopher Wren designed the Cathedral he had never seen a wheelchair, but two hundred were expected that day and somehow a way had to be found for them to enter the building. It was an extraordinary sight, this erection of scaffolding and wood, as it doubled back on itself in order to bring everyone to the floor level of this magnificent building, making it so easy for anyone in a wheelchair to get in.

Incidentally, three ramps were required in case of fire – or the roof falling in!

The Cathedral was packed when I got there. Twenty-seven of that vast congregation were members of the Groom family. We were each given a red rose, an anniversary brochure and an Order of Service, just in time as the service had practically started. Being in a wheelchair, my friend (an ex-Grooms artificial flower maker) was grandly escorted to the front by a steward, while I took my more lowly place at the back on the left hand side of the aisle. The Dean and Chapter, with the Bishop of Willesden, made their way to the West Door to greet Her Royal Highness The Duchess of Kent – for many years Patron of the Association. A great fanfare announced that she had arrived, and Charles Moore introduced her to members of the Council of Management. Not that I could see anything, being unfortunately lodged behind a pillar – but I could hear all the beautiful music and see the top of the Duchess' hat!

Great hymns were sung like: 'Praise to the Lord, the Almighty, the King of Creation' and 'Great is thy faithfulness'. Charles Moore told of John Groom's vision 125 years ago in the area around St Paul's and how that vision had grown, until today John Grooms Association is in the forefront of caring for disabled people in this country. Not only in the field of residential care but in housing and holidays, John Grooms is pre-eminent and all started by this young man's Christian commitment.

The choir sang Herbert Howell's setting of the 'Te Deum Laudamus' and this was followed by two readings, read in turn by Andrew Robertson and his wife Nancy. Andrew, who was a member of the Care Services Committee, read Psalm 138 and Nancy, who served on John Grooms Council for many years, read from St. Paul's letter to the Ephesians, ch. 3 vv. 14-20. Both being in wheelchairs, they had to read from the Choir floor since wheelchairs cannot climb lectern steps!

During the singing of 'Be thou my vision, O Lord of my heart' a collection of £5,431 was taken. This was to go exclusively towards the building of flats for physically disabled people. David Thompson, Chairman of the Association, then led the congregation in prayers from his wheelchair.

They were prayers for John Grooms – for Council, Staff and Volunteers – for Carers – for Residents and Tenants, asking rich blessing for all disabled people, God's strength in their weakness, His grace in their frustration and His encouragement to

HRH The Duchess of Kent arrives at St Paul's by the ramped entrance

participate more fully in every day life, to develop and extend their talents, and to make their own contribution in work, leisure, relationships and faith. Grooms have moved on over 125 years, but its spiritual ethos is still the same. The concluding words of the prayer could easily have been uttered by John Groom himself: 'Help us to change the things that need to be changed. Give us wisdom in the use of resources entrusted to us. Guide us in the decisions we need to make. Help us to share Your love with all people.'

As I joined in the service that day, listening – even if I couldn't see much that was going on! – I hadn't the remotest idea of the part I would yet be called to play in the life and work of John Grooms. In a previous chapter I mentioned I thought I had 'left' John Grooms when I gave up being a housemother – only to discover in the not too distant future Grooms hadn't left me! Far from it! When Grooms paved the way for disabled people to have anxiety-free holidays, my disabled friend became totally dependent upon them if she was to have a holiday at all. And I went with her.

Now here was the retiring President of the Association, Lord Coggan, giving the address and paying tribute to Charles Moore for his untiring work for John Grooms over the last twenty three years. Charles Moore would be retiring at the end of the year, and Lord Coggan welcomed the Rev. Michael Shaw, who would be taking his place, and wished him well. After eight years in the parochial ministry, in 1976 Michael moved from Redcar to the

Diocese of St. Albans, there to take an active role with the church's young people. He was responsible for a wide range of exciting and successful new initiatives within the Diocese including a new development, one of the first of its kind in the country, providing accessible canal holidays for children and young people with disabilities. From there it was just one step further to devote the whole of his ministry into caring for disabled people. And listening on that sunny April morning, I had no idea a vital link with Grooms was being forged again in my life.

I had met Charles Moore only a year previously. My friend and I had been staying at the Promenade Lodge at Minehead when Mr. Moore paid a visit there. He came and joined us just after breakfast one morning. He didn't have to, but he had evidently heard we were ex-John Grooms staff and made a point of speaking to us. That was the kind of caring man he was.

Discussing the years I had worked at Grooms and how happy and fulfilling they were – not only for me, but for many others who shared in that experience – I voiced my disappointment that no mention had been made of that particular period of time in the recently written book: 'In A Changing World' by Nancy Martin.

'Write it,' he said, without hesitation. 'Write it down,' he repeated decisively, 'and send it to me.' Which I did, believing his purpose was to gather as much material as he could to leave behind in the archives for posterity after his retirement.

I received a warm letter of acknowledgment and thanks, and for me that was the end of the matter – until some time later a further letter arrived from his secretary, Barbara Edwards, telling me the material had been taken out of the archives and some of it would be used in a new book that Charles Moore was going to write.

I was more than pleased when I heard this – not that some of my material would be used particularly, but because I believed Charles Moore to be just the man for bringing Grooms history up to date. I felt a strong urge to pray for the book – even more so when I discovered shortly after his retirement Charles began suffering a terminal illness.

As the months went past and I heard nothing more, I rang up to see if any progress was being made, and was devastated to learn that he had died the previous week. He had done an immense amount of research for the book but had only managed to draft the first few chapters before being overtaken by his illness.

Apart from being saddened by his death, there was the

The nave of St Paul's Cathedral, London – for JGADP 125th anniversary service

frustration. Why? Why the urge to pray – the urge that seems to come from deep inside and not manufactured of ourselves – when nothing was obviously going to come of it?

So when I received a letter from the Rev. Michael Shaw asking me if I would take on the writing of the history of John

Charles Moore retires – being presented with 'This Is Your Life' by the Rev Canon Roger Royle

Grooms, everything began to fall into place, and I am sure I felt a bit like Elisha must have done when inheriting Elijah's cloak, in my own strength unequal for the job, yet knowing as I stepped forward in faith I would find the ability. Also, I should like to feel it has been written partly in memory of Charles Moore, OBE, a great man of great character, whose strong Christian faith was the linchpin of his whole life and the motivating force behind all his work.

Paying tribute to Charles Moore, David Thompson, Chairman of John Grooms said:

'He was always ready to give an answer, a reason for the hope that was in him, But he did not ever parade his Christian faith. He believed that faith, if it did not have works, was dead and he sought by his works to show his faith. His faith was outstanding and, therefore, so were his works for disabled people.

The second quality was his integrity. I am reminded of the words which the historian, G. M. Trevelyan wrote about the early Quakers. He said "To maintain the Christian quality in the world of business and domestic life, and to retain it without pretension and hypocrisy, was the great achievement of these extraordinary people." That, too, has been the achievement of this extraordinary man. In all his dealings with the business side of Grooms he always manifested the dimension of complete integrity, earning the respect of everyone who met him.

The third, and perhaps the most outstanding characteristic, was his care and compassion, especially for disabled people. His favourite passage in the Bible was the story of how four friends of a paralytic man cared for him so much that they took the roof off a house in order to get him to Jesus. Scripture says that when Jesus saw their faith he said to the disabled man, "take up thy bed and walk." In like manner, Charles was prepared to move heaven and earth in order to help disabled people. To my mind, Charles' work was in the best tradition of the great 19th century reformers such as Lord Shaftesbury, Dr. Barnardo and George Muller. They were great pioneers and Charles perpetuated their ethic of care and compassion in his own generation amongst disabled people.'

A worthy eulogy indeed! But I am very conscious of owing a great deal to other people for the creation of this book – varied reports, personal histories and quotes, and especially to David Thompson for his tribute to Charles Moore and to David Harmer, Chief Executive of John Grooms Housing Association, for his report on housing.

Neither could this book have been written without the loyal support, help – and by no means least – fellowship of the Book Committee, comprising Nancy and Andrew Robertson, Barbara Edwards and Allan Plumpton. Each have their own personal testimony of their call to Grooms.

Andrew and Nancy Robertson are man and wife, both wheelchair users, and both living very active lives. Andrew has been on the Care Committee and also had the laborious task of editing this book. Nancy was invited to join the Grooms Council by Charles Moore and has only just retired from it. She has also served on the Care Services Committee and was Director of The Prince of Wales Advisory Group on Disability before retiring from it in 1990. She has just been awarded the MBE for all the service she has given the community. Both Nancy and Andrew have been deeply involved working for Church Action on Disability, which is a fellowship of men and women who work to translate the teachings of Christ into practical action in local, national and international affairs. The calling of both of them is clearly to serve disabled people.

Barbara Edwards is absolutely certain she was called to work at John Grooms. 'It all began in 1969,' she says. Barbara had her children to care for, and was looking for a job that would fit into school hours and school holidays. She had also settled, too, that the boundary of her search could not go beyond Finsbury Park. But the search went on for months without any success and, in the mood of resigning to the fact there was no job for her, she decided on a spring clean of the house – despite it being November! She had taken up the staircarpet one morning, and was deeply involved in her cleaning and thoroughly dishevelled in appearance, when the phone rang. It was the job agency advising her they thought there was a job that would suit her at Finsbury Park (John Grooms). Could she start at 2 p.m. that day? Her first reaction was to turn it down. It was already 12 o'clock and she felt she could never get herself ready and be there in time. But second thoughts prevailed. She downed tools, left everything just as it was, hoping that whoever arrived home first would be careful not to have an accident. Barbara was accepted by Grooms and started work, on a temporary basis, straight away sending out Christmas cards that had been ordered. What is more, Grooms wanted her to stay on in the New Year and allowed her to work the hours that suited her. She became secretary to Charles Moore – her services stretched to the full in later years – and retired in the summer of 1995, after a happy and full service of 25 years. Barbara has no hesitation in believing she had a special call to work for Grooms and has supplied me with a great deal of information for this book, and I am grateful.

Allan Plumpton FCA was appointed as Association Secretary in succession to Charles O'Connor in October 1976. He had been with John Grooms for a year, following twelve years of wide experience as a partner in a London firm of chartered accountants. He was, at that time, Chairman of the North London Group of the London and District Society of Chartered Accountants. His responsibilities now were the administration and finance of all aspects of the work of John Grooms – both the Charity and the Housing Association.

In 1981, as the scope of the work expanded still further, the Council decided to appoint him Director of Finance, and he continued as the Association Secretary. Allan held these positions until 1993, when he commenced a phased retirement, handing over the Secretaryship first to Reverend Philip Hodgins and the Finance Directorship to Andrew Whitehead ACA a year later.

Shortly before coming to Grooms, however, he had met with a nasty accident while fell walking. A bad fall laid him on his

Mr Eddie George, Governor of the Bank of England, collecting for John Grooms outside the Bank on St George's Day 1993

back for several weeks where deep thinking, divinely inspired, compelled him to change the direction of his career and work for other people, and a way quickly opened for him to come to Grooms. Allan also has supplied me with a considerable amount of detailed material and reports that I have been able to draw upon, and acting as escort to some of the Grooms complexes I have visited.

Lastly, but by no means least, I am grateful to Mr Paul Partridge who, in his Christian commitment, has proved a friend to Grooms by lending me a word processor, coming speedily to my rescue when it has proved problematical, willingly printing each chapter as it has been written, and transferring the finished material to the correct type of computer disk, ready for the printer.

I am deeply conscious that there are so many Friends of Grooms all over the country, who have cared and worked hard raising considerable sums of money, and the impossibility of being able to mention them all; staff of the past who have served Grooms so faithfully; staff who are currently serving the Association; well known personalities who have given freely of time, talent and service, known and unknown members of the public. After 130 years of Grooms existence, the list would be endless: I have attempted to keep right to the forefront the disabled clients themselves, their needs and how Grooms have been forerunners, throughout the years and into the future, fulfilling those needs. John Groom himself was moved by sheer compassion given to him by the Master he served. He gave no thought to himself and, however small or great the service rendered, undoubtedly these kindly friends of Grooms have been, and still are, motivated by the same compassion. Deeper than that, I believe that a Sovereign God – Who has a purpose for all our lives – plans for Grooms, whether those involved realise it or not. *Theirs is a rather special kind of service.*

EPILOGUE

Whenever an important move occurred for me at Grooms, it always seemed to happen in the Spring. It was the Spring of 1995 that saw me on a return visit to the Edgware Estate after many, many years away from it.

I had thought to see things vastly changed and was astonished with my very first glimpse to find it looked exactly the same. There was the same office block, with the same large unaltered factory building just beyond, the concert hall and the kitchen quarters. The only alteration I was to discover was that they were no longer used in the same way, or for the same purposes.

Only as I explored further did I see that there were changes on the site and − strangely to my mind biased by nostalgia − all for the better. I knew beforehand the lovely orchard had been cleared, the fruit trees that should now have been in full bloom cut down, and a whole area of it flattened to make a car park. I had thought it would look ugly and depressing, but it did not appear like that at all. Only a small portion had been tarmaced; fresh green grass flourished where the trees had been and the whole area had been delightfully landscaped. Right down at the bottom of the slope, near the stream that gave it its name, stood 'Brookside' with all the outward appearance and grace of a newly built country mansion and, despite being lower down than the older long standing houses, somehow dwarfing them into insignificance. Those same houses in which I had served appeared 'old and weary' beside this magnificent new building and, sadly it seemed, it would be a kindness to pull them down. Indeed Lilac where I had first served as assistant, had started collapsing of its own accord! Subsidence had finished it and it had had to be completely demolished.

The Nursing Home was still there, outwardly the same, but inwardly vastly improved. No danger now of a boiler blowing up, as in my time! It had been renamed 'The Beatrice Laing Care

Residents relaxing outside Brookside, Edgware

Centre' after the Laing family, who financed many improvements and have done so much for Grooms.

Roseway, where I had been housemother, had completely disappeared. A whole new Grooms housing complex bearing this name and stretching out into Stoneyfields Lane had taken its place, so that for a while, bewildered by its size, I could not quite get my bearings.

Chestnut, where I was to stay for the night, had been much improved both outwardly and inwardly. The dining room was almost unrecognisable from my time when oblong kitchen tables covered with white oil cloth had been part of its main furnishing, with meals sent in containers from the main kitchen, kept warm in the oven and served out by the housemother and her assistant when the girls came in from work. Now in their place were round stylish tables covered by a dainty cloth, shaded wall lights and a chef in the kitchen! Upstairs, too, each resident now had a self-contained flatlet as I had seen in other Grooms complexes.

I visited the 'Factory' that afternoon. No longer a factory, but known as the 'Resource Centre', I was greeted with a smile at the reception area by Sarah, one of the disabled residents and invited to sign my name. Opposite was a small shop presided over by another disabled resident. Pat Copley was in charge of the Centre and, as my disabled friend was with me, took us both on a conducted tour. Apart from the roses that Jane and Diane were working on ready for distribution on Grooms 130th anniversary, when to mark Grooms' historic link with London there was to be a St. George's Day breakfast reception at the Guildhall, there was no sign of the once famous artificial flowers. The various sized gophering irons and sand filled cushions, the pincers and veining machines once used in their construction were now housed behind the glass doors of a cabinet as museum pieces!

Several young men with various physical disabilities were engaged in fathoming the mystery – or delights – of computing, young women worked from their wheelchairs at embroidery, tapestry or painting. I understood all sorts of courses were on offer and also they could attend Hendon College for classes. Just to mention a few regular on-site activities: keep-fit, dressmaking, singing group, drama, music workshop, a Christian fellowship group, discussion group, woodworking, skills for independent living and cookery.

Post St George's Day breakfast at Guildhall 1995 – with some of the Groom family and present management group

Cookery instruction was being presently held in the basement, which had once been used as a cutting out and store room and for making dye and gum in the artificial flower making days. Now an appetising smell of baking was wafting up to us as we toured the top floor. It drew us like a magnet and, descending below, we found there a hive of activity round mixing bowls and ovens – both young men and women – with Austrian cheesecake being top of the menu.

Another activity now is pony-trapping. Transport is provided for a regular weekly trip to Napsbury, where those wanting to can take part in pony-trapping supervised by qualified and experienced staff.

Our next stop was at Brookside, a building that is not only a joy to look at outside, but a delight inside. Here we met up again after many years with a lady known as 'Goldie' – a shortened version of her surname who sadly recently passed away. We had known Goldie in our salad days at Grooms and although of course older, we found the same cheerful, sociable, companionable Goldie – offering us the hospitality of helping ourselves to anything we wished for our comfort. It was one incident, for me, that linked up completely and nostalgically with old times.

We stayed very comfortably in the Lady Laing flat – a flat reserved for visitors in Chestnut. It was good to meet up again

Ponytrapping at Napsbury

196

with Maud and Nancy, two of Grooms ladies from early days. After a night's rest I found myself waking up as dawn was approaching. I seemed drawn to look out of the window and, from that particular viewpoint, the landscape appeared no different from all those years ago. Except it was quiet. Of course no one expected it to be noisy at that time in the morning. But suddenly I found I could put my finger on the intangible element to this visit that had been eluding me. It had never been noisy on the Estate, even in my time, but there had always been the bustle of girls going to and from the factory during the day or out on their pursuits in the evening, best described, I suppose, as the 'hum of life.'

Now the houses of my time at Grooms stood empty, other buildings were not being used, pending redevelopment. The young people in the Resource Centre were only just learning where they wanted to go. The Estate, though peaceful, was in a transition period, poised for change as it moves towards the twenty-first century. Disabled people are challenged by more than one mountain to climb. And Grooms have a Destiny to lead the way. Your support, prayers and encouragement will ensure that they do.

Appendix A

TIME CHART

1845   John Groom is born in London.

1862   John Groom commenced apprenticeship.

1865   American Civil War ends.
        Woodbridge Free School built for 100 boys.

1866   Watercress and Flower Girls Mission established.

1867   John Groom successfully completed apprenticeship.

1868   John and Sarah Groom married on 5th March.

1870   Education Act – elementary education for all.

1879   Baroness Burdett-Coutts formed Flower Girls' Brigade.

1882   May Festival and Flower Show at Foresters Hall.

1883   Foresters Hall congregation of 900. Sunday School 500 children.

1885   Earl of Shaftesbury died.

1888   Three orphans fostered by John Groom's family.

1889   4,000 free breakfasts each week in winter. 800 halfpenny dinners.

1890   The start of the Clacton Homes. 52 girls in training for flower making.

1891   Rev Arthur Groom resigned as Assistant Secretary on appointment to pastorate in Sheffield.

1894   Church Fellowship moved to Woodbridge Chapel.

1895   100,000 free meals distributed in severe winter.

1896   F A Bevan became Treasurer.
        Woodbridge Sunday School ministry to 500 children.

1902   Local Education Authorities constituted.

1906   Grooms flowers decorate Mayoral banquet at Guildhall in London.

1908   First Children's Act passed.

1911   John Groom's Crippleage & Flower Girls Mission registered as a company limited by guarantee.
        Health and Unemployment Insurance first introduced.

1912   Haywards Place factory built. First Alexandra Day roses sold.

1914   First World War started.

1918   John Groom retired. Son Alfred appointed Secretary and Superintendent. First World War ended.

1919   John Groom died at Clacton. Buried in Highgate Cemetery.

1926   General Strike.

1931   Purchase of Edgware Estate.

1932   Official opening of Edgware Estate by Lord Mayor of London on 20th May.

1935   35,000 visited Clacton for Fete Days.

1939   Second World War started. Air raid shelters built at Edgware.

1942   Beveridge Plan published – the blueprint for the National Health Service.

1944   Education Act – secondary education for all.

1945   Second World War ends. Social Services introduced.
        Children's Homes moved to Kent.

1950-1965   Ruth Gillard worked at John Groom's Crippleage, Edgware.

1965   Stoneyfields House opened. The first young disabled male residents arrive at Edgware.

1966   100 years of John Grooms work.

1967   Office moved from Sekforde Street to Finsbury Park.

1969   Name changed to John Grooms Association for the Disabled.
First adapted wheelchair-accessible flat experiment (Finsbury Park).
John Grooms Housing Association (JGHA) founded.

1970   Geoffrey Parker House (Edgware) opened.

1973   JGHA's housing work began – Princess Crescent flats (London N4) opened.

1974   Holiday work began – Promenade Hotel (Minehead) purchased.

1976   London holiday flat opened.

1977   JGHA's second housing scheme at Whitby Court (London N7) opened – the start of an expanding housing development programme (see Appendix B)

1978   Stamford House (Thorpe Bay) closed and the last children in care transferred out for adoption or fostering.

1979   West Shore Hotel (Llandudno) opened. First 3 holiday caravans sited.

1979-1987   Ten additional self-catering holiday caravans, chalets and bungalows opened.

1981   International Year of Disabled People (IYDP).

1981-1983   Groomsmobile exhibition unit toured schools and groups throughout UK.

1983   HOPE Nursery set up at Cheshunt (Herts) employing 14 disabled horticultural workers (official opening in April 1984).

1984   Dolphin Court residential (& training) home at Thorpe Bay opened.

1985   'Activities Centre' at Edgware opened, including ATW programme.

1988   John Grooms Court Norwich residential (& training) home opened.

1989-1990   Three small long-stay residential homes opened in the Southend area in conjunction with Southend Health Authority following hospital closures.

1990   Name changed to John Grooms Association for Disabled People.
Jane Hodge Hotel, near Cowbridge (S Wales) opened.
'Treetops' (Colchester) nursing/residential care home opened.

1991   125th anniversary service.

1992   Extension to Jane Hodge Hotel opened. Community Care agency service opened at Colchester.
Silver Birches, residential unit at Finsbury Park converted into additional office space for rapidly growing head office staff.

1993   Mardon House (Exeter) opened. Management subsequently transferred to Exeter and District NHS Trust.

1994   Community Care agency service opened at Cowbridge (S Wales).
25th anniversary service of JGHA.

1995   Edgware redevelopment planning application submitted to local authority.

1996   Head Office moved from Finsbury Park to Scrutton Street, EC2.
John Grooms publish their book, *More Than One Mountain to Climb*, commemorating their 130th anniversary year.

Appendix B

JOHN GROOMS HOUSING ASSOCIATION
HOUSING SCHEMES UNDER MANAGEMENT

At 31 December 1995 there were 817 units being managed by JGHA
as listed below:

		Number of Units	
	Date Scheme Opened	Wheelchair & Special Needs	General Needs (inc. Warden)
Locations			
Princess Crescent, London N4	1973	12	1
Whitby Court, London N7	1977	12	–
Hanover/Ross Court, London NW9	1981	12	2
Davenport Lodge, Heston, Middx		19	1
The Orchard, Edgware, Middx	1982	6	2
The Firs, Stoneyfields Lane, Edgware	1983	6	3
Whiteside Lodge, Henleaze, Bristol		15	18
Brookdene Lodge, Swindon, Wilts		18	18
Clarkes Way, Houghton Regis, Dunstable	1984	23	23
Waltham Lodge, Leyton, E10	1985	6	4
Maes Trisant, Llantrisant, Mid Glam		30	1
Wylye Lodge, Wilton, Salisbury, Wilts	1986	26	1
Ash Close, Edgware, Middx		22	11
Groomside, South Street, Braintree, Essex	1987	16	6
Bramston Close, Hainault, Essex		23	9
Grooms Drive, Hillingdon, Middx	1989	30	1
Trenchard Lodge, Chelmsford, Essex		40	2
Kinlett Close, Colchester, Essex		6	6
Castle Court, Thornbury, Avon	1990	14	14
Shaw House, Caterham, Surrey	1992	–	17
Queens Park Road, Caterham, Surrey		–	6
The Grange, Warlingham, Surrey		–	7
Coulsdon Road, Caterham, Surrey		–	2
Peel Close, Chingford, London E4		6	–
Charles Moore Court, Polegate		7	14
Roseway, Edgware, Middx	1993	10	20

	Date Scheme Opened	Number of Units	
		Wheelchair & Special Needs	General Needs (inc. Warden)
Locations			
Ash Close, Phase II, Edgware, Middx	1993	11	17
Brookside, Edgware, Middx		23	–
Mali Jenkins House, Walsall, W Midlands		19	1
Kent House, Stoke Mandeville, Aylesbury	1994	20	1
Old School Close, Polegate, E Sussex		9	13
Jacobs Close, Stantonbury, Milton Keynes		14	–
Highwoods, Colchester, Essex		10	–
Lerwick Drive, Slough, Berkshire		2	–
Millview Meadows, Rochford, Essex		8	11
Tara Close, Colchester, Essex		2	–
Acorn Gardens, Birmingham	1994	5	–
St Andrew's Road, Birmingham		2	–
Sandiford House, Caterham	1995	3	13
Dyers Mews, Milton Keynes		6	9
Ashway, Beach Road, Birmingham		1	–
Churchill Road, Caterham, Surrey		2	–
Headway Court, Rusthall, Tunbridge Wells		8	–
Mersea Road, Colchester, Essex		2	2
Queens Road, Southend, Essex		1	–
Court Drive, Wellington, Somerset		8	–
Forest Park Avenue, Clacton, Essex		1	–
St John's, Hackney, London N4		14	26
Malthouse Road, Portsmouth, Hants		1	–
Weald Court, Lewes, Sussex		2	–
Forest Park Avenue, Clacton, Essex		1	–
Southacre Avenue, Birmingham		1	–
Totals		535	282

Total number of units under management   817

SCHEMES UNDER CONSTRUCTION

At the end of 1995 there were a further 140 units in 29 different locations either under construction or 'in the pipeline', as follows:

Completion expected by early 1997

	Wheelchair & Special Needs	General Needs	Total
Birmingham	9	–	
Bromley, Kent	2	–	
Camden, London NW1	7	–	
Hillingdon, Middx	9	–	
Hoveton, N Norfolk	1	1	
Letchworth, Herts	9	12	
Milton Keynes	2	–	
Newbury, Berks	5	–	
Peterborough, Northants	6	–	
Redbridge, London	2	–	
Sandwell, W Midlands	4	–	
Southend, Essex	7	–	
Taunton, Somerset	2	–	
Tunbridge Wells, Kent	14	8	
Tunstead, N Norfolk	1	1	
Uttlesford, Essex	2	–	
	82	22	104

Completion expected by early 1998

	Wheelchair & Special Needs	General Needs	Total
Adur, W Sussex	2	–	
Birmingham	1	–	
Bristol	3	–	
Colchester, Essex	2	–	
Dover, Kent	2	–	
Hertsmere, Herts	1	–	
Hillingdon, Middx	6	–	
Hove, E Sussex	1	–	
Milton Keynes	2	–	
Portsmouth	2	1	
Redbridge, London	3	–	
Tandridge, Surrey	2	–	
Wandsworth, London	8	–	
	35	1	36
Total	117	23	140

Appendix C

JOHN GROOMS LEADERSHIP
(John Grooms Association for Disabled People)

PAST OFFICE HOLDERS:

Presidents

1866–1885	The 7th Earl of Shaftesbury
1889–1893	The Earl of Aberdeen
1936–1953	The Lord Radstock
1963–1991	The Rt Rev & Rt Hon The Lord Coggan of Canterbury & Sissinghurst, MA DD

Chairmen

1900–1911	Mr Peter Rigby Pratt
1912–1920	Mr Herbert Clarkson
1921–1929	Mr E C Emmerson
1930–1933	Mr Edward Cooke
1934	Mr E J Lovell
1935–1936	Various members of Council
1937	Mr A Matthews
1938–1939	Mr B Ewart White, JP
1939–1940	Mr F J Stradwick
1940–1945	Mr A Gordon Lovell
1945–1947	Mr Arnold S Clark
1947–1949	Mr A Matthews
1949–1960	Mr Alec Daines
1960–1970	Mr Arnold S Clark
1970–1981	Mr F H Willows, FCIS FCCA
1981–1989	His Honour Judge Hitching

Treasurers

1885–1896	Mr Thomas Johnson
1896–1919	Mr F A Bevan
1920–1938	Mr Ernest J Lovell
1938–1960	Mr A Gordon Lovell
1960–1968	Mr J B Calder, FCA
1968–1970	Mr F H Willows, FCIS FCCA
1970–1974	Mr Arnold S Clark, JP
1974–1985	Mr R Taylor, FCA
1985–1995	Mr Derrick T Rodgers, FCA

Superintendents/Principals/Executive Directors

1866–1918	Mr John A Groom
1918–1932	Mr Alfred G Groom
1932–1944	Mr Edward Cooke
1946–1966	Mr Geoffrey Parker
1966–1976	The Rev Alfred C S Bell
1976–1992	Mr Charles H Moore, OBE

Secretaries

1866–1918	Mr John A Groom
1918–1944	Mr Alfred G Groom
1944–1976	Mr Charles O'Connor, MBE
1976–1993	Mr Allan L Plumpton, FCA

PRESENT OFFICE HOLDERS (January 1996):

Patron:
HRH The Duchess of Kent

President:
The Most Rev & Rt Hon Dr George Carey, The Archbishop of Canterbury

Life President:
The Rt Rev & Rt Hon The Lord Coggan of Canterbury & Sissinghurst, MA DD

Vice-Presidents:
Mr Peter Barkworth
Mr Andrew Buxton
Lady Mary Clayton
Mrs Norma Major
Mr D F Ellison Nash, OBE FRCS
His Honour Judge Hitching
Mrs P M Hobson, JP
Sir Maurice Laing
Professor Lord McColl of Dulwich
Miss Esther Rantzen, OBE
Mrs Nancy Robertson, MBE
The Rev Canon Roger Royle, AKC
The Rt Rev David Sheppard, Bishop of Liverpool
The Rt Hon Viscount Tonypandy, PC DCL
Miss Jill Turner

JOHN GROOMS LEADERSHIP
(John Grooms Association for Disabled People)

PRESENT OFFICE HOLDERS (January 1996) – continued

Chairman:
Mr D H Thompson, LLB

Council of Management:
Mr A W Bush, JP LLB FRSA (Joint Vice-Chairman)
Mr K Barnes, CBE
Mrs G Y Fairweather, Dip COT (Joint Vice-Chairman)
Mr P N Griffiths, FCA (Hon Treasurer)
Mrs R Griffiths
Miss V G Howarth
Miss P Liddiard
Mrs M McCabe Neil
Mrs J Pacheco
Mr J Rawding
The Rev Canon Roger Royle, AKC
Mr R Scott
Mr M Smith, FCA
Miss D Sugden
Miss J Turner
Mr J Wheatley

Honorary Advisers:
Hon Medical Adviser:
    Mr J D Griffiths, MS FRCS
Hon Financial Adviser:
    Mr C D Carr, BSc FCA

Executive Officers:
Executive Director:
    The Rev R M Shaw, DipAdEd
Director of Finance:
    Mr A P Whitehead, ACA
Director of Services & Development:
    Mr D R Newnham, CQSW
Director of Fundraising & Public Relations:
    Mr K J Wenden, MICFM
Company Secretary:
    The Rev P A Hodgins, MBA MIPD

JOHN GROOMS LEADERSHIP
(John Grooms Housing Association)

PAST OFFICE HOLDERS:

Chairmen
1969–1981	Mr Frank H Willows, FCCA
1981–1982	Mr Alan N Hitching, MA BCL
1982–1985	Mr Michael E Follett, FRICS
1985–1990	Mr Paul Reynolds, ARIBA

Directors/Chief Executives
1969–1976	Mr Charles O'Connor
1977–1988	Mr Charles H Moore

Secretaries
1969–1976	Mr Charles O'Connor
1976–1977	Mr Charles H Moore
1977–1990	Mr Allan L Plumpton, FCA

PRESENT OFFICE HOLDERS (January 1996):

Chairman
Mr E W J Picton, FCA ATII

Committee of Management
Mr J Davis
Mr R Grove, ARICS
Mr C R Joyce, FRICS ACIArbMBIM
Mr P Reynolds, ARIBA
Mr J T Robertson, FCIS
Mrs S Ruddick
Mr A T Shephard
Mr J T Smith, MBIFM MAPM
Mr D H Thompson, LLB
Mr D E H Titheradge, FCA

Executive Officers
Chief Executive:
    Mr D J Harmer
Secretary and Director of Finance:
    Mr A R W Beattie, FCA
Development Manager:
    Mr R W Souster, BSc CEng MICE
Housing Manager:
    Mr J M Robertson, BA MCIH
Maintenance Manager:
    Mr M Wilton, AIMBM